DISCOVER·●·NATURE
in the
Weather

DISCOVER · NATURE

in the
Weather

Things to Know and Things to Do

Tim Herd
with illustrations by Patrice Kealy

STACKPOLE
BOOKS

To my parents, Joe and Rusty Herd, with thanks.

Published by
STACKPOLE BOOKS
5067 Ritter Road
Mechanicsburg, PA 17055
www.stackpolebooks.com

Printed in the United States of America

First edition

10 9 8 7 6 5 4 3 2 1

Cover illustrations by Patrice Kealy
Cover design by Wendy A. Reynolds

Library of Congress Cataloging-in-Publication Data

Herd, Tim.
   Discover nature in the weather / Tim Herd.
     p. cm.
   ISBN 0-8117-2716-5
   1. Meteorology. 2. Weather. I. Title.

QC861.2 .H46 2001
551.5—dc21

00-032958

CONTENTS

INTRODUCTION

Discover Nature in the Weather is about observing, about learning and under-standing, and about enjoying the constant panorama of an ever-changing sky scrolling by. At once awesome and fearsome, the weather is always a source of inspiration and an invitation to discovery.

On these pages, the inquiring mind may find a new truth here or there. Yet truths themselves are not really new; it is just that we are only now com-prehending the true workings of weather and how it applies to our lives and to those of our co-inhabitants of the unique planet with the skin of air and water.

HOW TO USE THIS BOOK

I invite you to an adventure in discovery. Use this book to develop an under-standing of the processes, the mechanisms, and the two-way interactions we share with the atmosphere.

Discover Nature in the Weather presents these concepts in a well-organized, easy-to-understand manner, combining aspects of a readable meteorology text, a useful field reference, and an enjoyable introduction to making practical observation and performing hands-on experiments. Accompanying the text are drawings, diagrams, and maps to further interpret the forces of the observable sky. Tables and charts provide information for estimating wind force and wind chill, comparing the effects of heat and humidity, formulating forecasts, preparing for weather extremes and natural disasters, and much more.

ACTIVITIES

But the book isn't all just facts and information. The thrill of weather is in our experience of the it. The end of each chapter offers a variety of observations to make, experiments to perform, and things to do, using common household items or readily available, inexpensive equipment. Identify clouds and gauge their movements. Keep a daily weather observation log. Photograph the changing skies. Measure the acidity of rainwater. Track a hurricane.

As you read, you'll see that a tremendous variety of units are in common use to quantify the natural world. An international system of units based on the metric system is the accepted standard of science and industry. Yet because most nonscientists in the United States find them unfamiliar (the United States and Burma are the only countries that do not use the metric system for their principal measure!), the book uses the U.S. conventional system in most cases. Conversion factors for all the units are listed in Appendix 1.

ADDITIONAL RESOURCES

The appendices also offer a selected bibliography and lists of sources for weather information and products. The Internet is a tremendous resource for weather and climatological data—and as much extra data and minutia as your input appetite craves. But remember that anybody can put stuff on the Internet. Not everything you find is truth. Stick with the governmental agencies, universities, and respected companies for the critical stuff; compare and check dubious info with other sources for confirmation.

Throughout the book, the drawings of Patrice Kealy succeed in capturing the ceaseless motion of that ethereal mixture of air and a little water that is our atmosphere. And you may want to emulate her. A good observer takes notes, makes sketches, diagrams movements, and analyzes situations: document your weather experiences. Keep a camera handy, too.

You will soon learn that the real stuff of weather is not found in a book. For that, you'll want to get outside and discover nature on your own. Observe, marvel, and enjoy.

CHAPTER 1

Air:
The Sky's the
Limit

Without the special stuff that is air, there would be no atmosphere hospitable to life on this planet. Air smothers the surface of the earth so densely that we may breathe it with ease. Insects, the most plentiful of all creatures, do not even need special muscles to pull it into their bodies, but rather allow oxygen to be absorbed directly from the air into their tissues. Plants utilize air in both respiration for life and food production for growth.

The atmosphere, with its unique proportion and mixture of gases, water, dust, and airborne particulates, is a thin, transparent skin adhering to the surface of the blue planet, bonded only by gravity. Warmed with just the right amount of heat, and stirred into motion by the sun, it transports moisture about the globe. The atmosphere insulates, protects, and sustains life on earth.

ATMOSPHERIC COMPOSITION

Custom-designed for earth and its inhabitants, our atmosphere is a unique combination of chemically distinct gases that make life possible and weather interesting. Nitrogen is the largest component, 78.1 percent, followed by oxygen, at 20.9 percent, argon at .93 percent, and carbon dioxide with just .04 percent. Other gases making up the remaining tiny percent of the atmosphere include traces (in decreasing amounts) of neon, helium, ozone, methane, krypton, hydrogen, nitrous oxide, carbon monoxide, nitrogen oxides, ammonia, sulfur oxides, and other trace gases.

Most of these gases do not measurably vary in proportion according to time or place. Ozone, however, which plays a vital role in absorbing ultraviolet radiation, varies with height, latitude, and season. And gases affected by living organisms also vary—gases such as carbon dioxide and methane—as they are removed from or released into the atmosphere. The concentration of carbon dioxide, for example, decreases each year during the growing season as plants engage it in photosynthesis, and it increases in the hemisphere's winter.

> **FACT: The green plants of earth withdraw about forty billion tons of carbon dioxide per year from the atmosphere.**

In this mixture of gases are suspended small amounts of water and dust, which can vary in concentration. Water vapor can be as low as near zero percent to as high as 3 or 4 percent, depending on rates of evaporation, condensation and precipitation, and presence of clouds. Its presence has a profound influence on weather. Dust, or *particulate matter,* in the air influences short-term weather as well as long-term climates and surface conditions.

ATMOSPHERIC PROFILE

The atmosphere is pulled toward the center of the earth by gravity. The pressure of the gases, however, resists such a pull, pushing outward toward space. The result is a quite slender sphere of air surrounding the globe, densest at the surface, tapering off to where individual molecules of gas do not even meet each other, then to the nothingness in space.

Because of this gradual tapering, we cannot say exactly how thick the atmosphere is. But we can talk about its density. Fifty percent of its mass lies less than 3.5 miles above sea level; 90 percent of it is within about 10 miles, and 99.9 percent is below 29 miles. Even at a height of 350 miles, however, air has been detected, although its density there is about one-trillionth of that at sea level.

While there are no distinct boundaries on the atmosphere, it is helpful to think of it existing in layers based on the average vertical variation of temperature. The lowest, thinnest, but densest layer is the *troposphere,* containing about 80 percent of the total mass of the atmosphere and virtually all the action of the weather. It is where tremendous mixing occurs and much upward and downward motion of air.

Temperature tends to decrease with height in the troposphere. This temperature decrease averages 18°F per vertical mile and is called the *environmental lapse rate.* A second type of lapse rate occurs as air moves upward, expands and cools, and is called the *adiabatic lapse rate,* which varies with the concentration of water vapor: 1°C/100 m (5.4°F/1000 feet) for dry air and .5°C/100 m (3°F/1000 ft.) for moist air. At times in small and shallow portions, the temperature in the troposphere can be constant with height. The temperature may even rise with height, and this is called an *inversion.*

The top of the troposphere, where temperature no longer decreases with height, is called the *tropopause,* forming the boundary between the troposphere and the stratosphere. This area averages 6.8 to 7.5 miles above sea level, but may be anywhere between 4.3 to 5.0 miles in the polar regions and 10 to 11 miles in the tropics. Perhaps surprisingly, the coldest temperatures in the tropopause (−90°F or colder) occur over the tropics, where the tropopause is higher, rather than over the poles, where it is lower (and temperatures drop to only −40°F).

The tropopause is not always one continuous boundary. Often the tropopause above the tropics extends outward to about 30° latitude, where it breaks off and continues poleward at a lower level. Near the poles, the tropopause slopes downward toward the surface and may show another break. Often occupying the vertical space between such breaks, where the troposphere and stratosphere mix, are the powerful wind currents known as jet streams.

Extending above the tropopause to a height of 31 miles or so is the *stratosphere,* where temperature increases with height, up to 32°F—and sometimes even as high as 68°F. This increase is due to the presence of ozone, which absorbs heat in the form of ultraviolet radiation from the sun. This temperature profile—warmer over colder—inhibits vertical mixing and leads to a stable, stratified distribution of air, hence the layer's name.

The air here is very dry, which makes clouds very rare. Occasionally the tops of tall thunderstorms may penetrate the lower part of the stratosphere. At the *stratopause*—the very top of the stratosphere—air pressure is a mere one-thousandth of that at sea level.

Above the stratopause is the remaining one tenth of 1 percent of the atmosphere's mass. Almost all of that fraction is at home in the *mesosphere,* or middle atmosphere. At this altitude, the ozone has thinned to the point where it no longer absorbs heat. Heat is now radiated out to space, and the temperature again decreases with height—to about –130°F at the *mesopause,* the very top of the mesosphere, some 53 to 56 miles up. Despite the extreme low density of its air, the mesosphere has the distinction of announcing meteors to the world, visibly igniting their surfaces by the heat of friction with the sparse air molecules.

The mesopause gives way to the *thermosphere,* in which the temperature rises once again due to the gases' absorption of the extremely short ultraviolet waves of the sun's radiation. Temperatures climb as high as 180°F. The upper thermosphere is where many man-made satellites orbit. Despite the sparse air, these satellites still experience atmospheric drag that can eventually bring them down to incinerate in the lower atmosphere.

Above the poles, the thermosphere hosts the displays of *auroras,* when particles from the sun excite the gases into glowing. The top boundary of the thermosphere, the *thermopause,* exists more in name than in reality. It is estimated to be between 300 to 600 miles high and can change radically with the amount of sunlight reaching it.

Embedded within the thermosphere is the *ionosphere,* a region where atoms have become ionized—charged by the loss or gain of an electron by ultraviolet radiation. The ionosphere itself is subdivided into layers based on varying effects on radio waves. Radio waves can be bounced around the earth

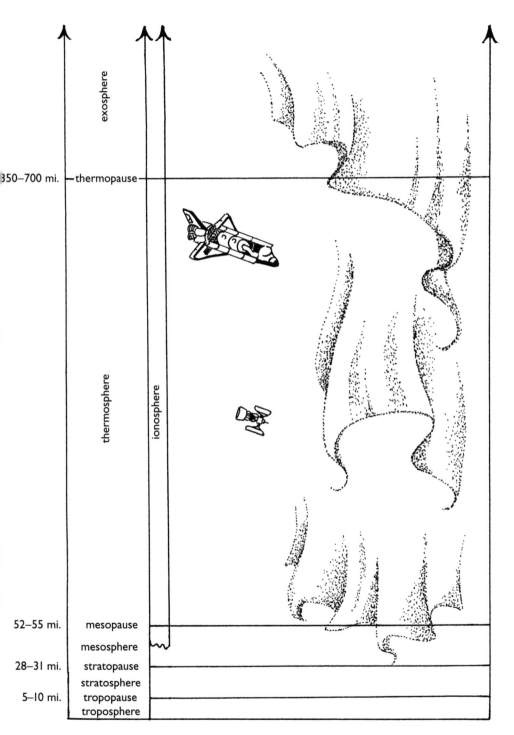

exosphere

350–700 mi. — thermopause —

thermosphere

ionosphere

52–55 mi. mesopause

mesosphere

28–31 mi. stratopause

stratosphere

5–10 mi. tropopause

troposphere

Atmosphere Profile

THE HEAT'S ON

The U.S. space shuttle has a way to beat the heat of high-speed reentry into earth's atmosphere. The shuttle orbits the earth at 17,000 mph at heights between 100 and 600 miles. As the shuttle reenters the atmosphere on its way back to earth, the friction from bumping into the sparse gases of the upper atmosphere creates temperatures between 1300°F and 2400°F. NASA devised a heat shield to dissipate the high heat and prevent the shuttle from becoming an expensive and deadly man-made meteor. The shield consists of 24,100 black tiles and 6,800 white tiles made from a porous insulative material of high-purity silica fibers coated with borosilicate glass. The material's heat conductivity is so poor that when one side of a tile is heated white-hot, the other side is cool enough to touch bare-handed.

through the ionosphere at predetermined angles, eliminating the problem of the earth's curvature in long-range communications.

FACT: It's lonely at the top. In the vacuum of space at 200 miles up, a single molecule of gas may travel a mile before it encounters any other gas molecule.

Whatever's left of the atmosphere above the thermopause is called the *exosphere.* Gas molecules are so rare they may not even collide with each other, and some may even slip the bonds of earth entirely and leave gravity behind. In the exosphere, atmospheric gases give way to the magnetic fields and radiation belts of outer space.

WEATHER INGREDIENTS

A number of factors contribute to bringing the morning's weather to our continent and doorstep. The density of air not only varies with height in the atmosphere, but is also dependent on the amount of heat in the air. Warmer air is less dense than cooler air, and flows from areas of higher pressure to lower pressure, causing wind. Factor in the moisture component of the atmosphere, and you've got the ingredients for weather: atmospheric pressure, moisture, and heat.

Atmospheric Pressure. In visualizing atmospheric pressure, it's convenient to speak of an imaginary column of air extending from a certain level up through the entire height of the atmosphere. And though this imaginary column has no walls, the concept helps us understand atmospheric pressure as the weight of all the air above that level.

The weight is the total mass of all the air in the column, where the number of molecules in the thin air of the upper atmosphere is far less per unit volume than the number in compressed air at the surface. The higher you go, the less air there is above you, the less the weight per unit area, hence the less air pressure.

Pressure is not the result of the density of air alone, however. Enter heat and its influences. The pressure of a contained gas can be increased by adding heat. The opposite is also true; for example, if we put an inflated balloon in the refrigerator, its size shrinks because its internal pressure decreases. But remember that the atmosphere is not so contained, and the density of the air is free to

RANGES OF RECORDED ATMOSPHERIC PRESSURE

	Millibars	Inches of Mercury	Location	Date
Highest recorded sea level pressure	1084	32.01	Agata, Siberia	Dec. 31, 1968
Very strong high pressure area	1050	31.00		
Moderate high pressure area	1030	30.42		
Mean sea level pressure	1013.25	29.92		
Moderate low pressure area	995	29.39		
Very strong low pressure area	976	28.82		
Hurricane Gilbert	888	26.23	Gulf of Mexico	Sept. 14, 1988
Typhoon Tip; lowest recorded sea level pressure	870	25.66	Pacific Ocean	Oct. 12, 1979

PRESSURE POINTS

Atmospheric pressure is the force exerted on the earth's surface by the atmosphere. The unit of measurement to express that force is the bar, normally expressed in the United States in *millibars,* where 1000 millibars (mb) equals 1 bar. We also speak of *inches of mercury,* derived from reading the height of the column in a barometer. When we refer to 30 inches, what we're really saying is the atmospheric pressure is enough to support a column of mercury 30 inches high. To convert: 1 inch of mercury (Hg) = 33.86 mb; 30 inches of mercury = 1016 mb.

vary with a change in temperature. As air warms, it also expands, taking up more room with the same amount of air molecules, which decreases its density. Factor in the differences in temperatures at different levels of the atmosphere, which may all be moving in different directions vertically and horizontally, and we begin to see why predicting the weather is at once so fascinating and so challenging.

As we measure the atmospheric pressure—the weight of the air in the "column" above us—we find it changes almost continuously, corresponding with how much air is moving over us and how the air is affected by daily and seasonal heating and cooling cycles. Generally speaking, lower pressure areas are associated with cloudiness, precipitation, and storms, and higher pressure areas with fair weather and clearer skies.

Moisture. Although water exists in the atmosphere in all three phases—solid, liquid, and vapor—it is the vapor form that has the most influence on weather. Its transport around the globe, its interaction and distribution among living and nonliving resources, and its constant phase changes are all part of the *hydrologic cycle* (see chapter 3).

The concentration of vapor varies enormously with height, latitude and longitude, and time, and is the trickiest variable to measure and to predict the consequences of. In the tropics, near the ocean surface, water vapor makes up almost 4 percent of the atmosphere by volume; but up 10 miles or so, near the tropopause, water vapor drops to about 3 parts per million by volume. The concentration of water vapor in the air is often expressed as *relative humidity,* a comparative measure of how much vapor is present to how much is possible.

Water in the air is a major factor in many atmospheric chemical reactions that lead to hydroxyl and other radicals that destroy ozone and assist in producing the acids of air pollution. But water's greatest effect on the weather comes from its content of energy. Water is a high absorber of infrared radiation and involves large amounts of energy in its constant phase changes between vapor, liquid, and ice. These changes have the important result of affecting the heat balance in the atmosphere.

Heat. Heat fuels the weather engine. Without it, the atmosphere would stratify and calm, and weather—and life itself—would cease. Its relative absence is defined as cold. Temperature is the measure of heat, which is determined by the speed of the molecules of a substance. Heat itself is a form of energy that can be transferred from one object to another: The greater the energy, the greater the temperature.

In the atmosphere, heat is transferred by radiation, conduction, and convection.

FACT: Maple sap flows best on the south side of the tree, where it is first warmed by the sun.

Radiation. *Radiation* is energy transmitted via electromagnetic waves. Everything that has a temperature (and therefore heat) both emits and absorbs radiation. The higher the temperature, the more radiation it emits; the lower the temperature, the less radiation it gives off. The sun, being very hot, gives off a tremendous amount of radiation in the wavelengths of visible

---

TAKING A TEMPERATURE

Temperature is simply the measure of heat. Everything down to the subatomic level that moves has heat, and therefore a temperature.

The instrument used to measure heat is the thermometer, invented by Galileo in 1593. The most common thermometers use mercury or alcohol sealed in a glass tube marked with gradations. Both these liquids freely expand and contract with the amount of heat, and remain unfrozen in the biggest part of the air temperature range on earth.

---

light; the earth, being much cooler than the sun, emits much less radiation, and at much longer wavelengths than visible light.

If an object or surface receives more radiation than it gives off, it warms; if it emits more than it receives, it cools. The balance is partly a function of surface characteristics. For example, an asphalt parking lot, dark in color, absorbs much more incoming solar radiation than does a fresh covering of snow. The white snow reflects most of the visible light radiation back into the

---

INVENTING SCALES

The Fahrenheit temperature scale was developed by physicist Gabriel Fahrenheit (1686–1736). Although thermometers had been invented earlier, no standard scale was used to compare works between scientists until Fahrenheit developed the one that bears his name. It is most widely used in the United States. It is designated by °F.

The Celsius scale is named after its developer, Anders Celsius, a Swedish astronomer (1701–1744), and is the most widely used scale throughout the rest of the world. Its original designation, the centigrade scale, was replaced in nomenclature by degrees Celsius in 1948 at the Ninth General Conference on Weights and Measures. Its designation is °C.

Both the Fahrenheit and Celsius scales use the freezing and boiling points of water as reference points. Fahrenheit uses a smaller degree size than Celsius, dividing the difference between freezing and boiling into 180 degrees (from 32 degrees for freezing to 212 for boiling). Celsius divides the difference into 100 degrees (from 0 degrees for freezing to 100 for boiling).

The Kelvin scale is commonly used throughout the world by scientists, and was developed by the British scientist William Thomson, Lord Kelvin (1824–1907). It is designated by K alone (without the degree sign).

The Kelvin is an *absolute temperature scale,* basing its reference point on absolute zero, or the complete absence of heat—absolutely no molecular motion. This point is designated 0 degrees. The Kelvin scale, originally called the absolute scale, uses the same degree size as Celsius. On the Kelvin scale, the freezing point of water is at 273 degrees and the boiling point is at 373.

atmosphere, while absorbing very little. (Chapter 2 deals more with incoming solar radiation and its influences.)

Conduction. *Conduction* is the transfer of heat within or between substances at the molecular level, from molecule to molecule, always flowing from an area with higher temperature to one with lower temperature. The rate of conduction depends on the temperature difference (the larger the difference, the faster the heat flow) and on the material (metals are good conductors of heat, the air is a very poor conductor).

Molecules of hot chocolate, vibrating very fast, collide with the molecules of a cold metal cup, causing them to vibrate faster, which in turn causes the molecules in one's fingers to vibrate faster, transferring—or conducting—heat from the chocolate to the metal cup to the fingers. This is done quite quickly,

---

A MATTER OF DEGREES

Here's how to convert between the principal temperature scales: Celsius, Fahrenheit, and Kelvin. To convert from Fahrenheit to Celsius, subtract 32, then multiply by .556. To convert from Celsius to Fahrenheit, multiply by 1.8, then add 32. To convert from Celsius to Kelvin, add 273.

	Kelvin	Celsius	Fahrenheit
Boiling point, water	373	100	212
Boiling point, alcohol	351.5	78.5	173.2
Highest recorded shade temp. Al'azizyah, Libya, Sept. 13, 1922	331	58.0	136.4
Average human body temp.	310	58.0	98.6
Freezing/melting point, water	273	0	32
Freezing/melting point, ocean water	270	–3	27
Freezing/melting point, mercury	235.4	–37.7	–38.7
Freezing/sublimating point, carbon dioxide	194.3	–78.7	–109.7
Lowest recorded air temp. Vostok, Antarctica, July 21, 1983	184	–89.6	–128
Freezing/melting point, alcohol	155.9	–117.3	–179
Absolute zero	0	–273.15	–459.69

and quite effectively, as those who have burned their fingers on a metal cup can testify. On the other hand, air's poor conductive quality has been put to practical use in double-and triple-paned windows, where a layer of air between the glass insulates from the cold outdoors.

Conduction has little effect on weather. Even if the ground gets very hot, the air above it does not warm by conduction more than for just the bottom few inches. Conduction of heat occurs more easily in solids and liquids, where molecules are vibrating closer together than they are in gases.

AWAY WITH MERCURY

Common thermometers and barometers use alcohol or mercury to gauge changes in heat and pressure, but other types do not. Called *aneroid,* meaning without liquid, they simply use different materials to sense the changes.

A bimetal thermometer works with a coiled strip of two different metals fixed together. As heat is applied, the different metals expand at different rates, moving a pointer on a calibrated dial. Large-dial outdoor thermometers and oven thermometers work on this principle.

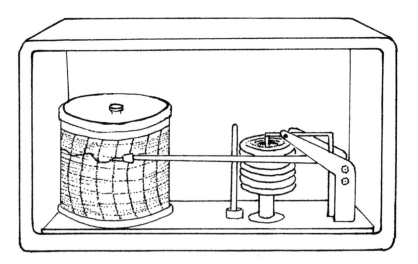

Aneroid Barometer. An aneroid barometer senses atmospheric pressure by using a vacuum chamber, to which is attached a lever and gears to transmit changes to a pointer on a dial. A barograph is an aneroid barometer that uses a pen to record the changes on a rotating chart.

FACT: The coldest annual mean temperature is found at the Pole of Inaccessibility, Antarctica: −72°F.

Convection. *Convection* is the transfer of heat by movement through a fluid or gas. Convection of heat cannot occur in solids, but only in a fluid or gas in which currents occur, where heat flows along with the movement of the fluid or gas itself.

Convection in the atmosphere happens in any and all directions currents occur. In practice, however, we use different terms to identify the various directions of heat flow via currents. Convection is reserved for upward motion. *Subsidence* is used to refer to downward transfer of heat. Horizontal convection is known as *advection,* and is brought by the wind flowing in a direction in which there is a change in the local temperature.

EFFECTS OF EARTH'S MOTIONS

Heat, pressure, and moisture, while major internal contributors to the behavior of the atmosphere, are not the only ones. The atmosphere swaddles a rotating, revolving planet with its own motions and cycles, directed by the sun and moon. These external forces exert themselves in both major and minor ways.

The earth revolves about the sun in an elliptical orbit that is almost circular. The minimum distance between the earth and sun *(perihelion)* occurs about January 3 each year; the maximum distance *(aphelion)* occurs about July 4. Obviously (one may think) January should be warmer than July. But this is also obviously not the case, at least in the northern hemisphere. Seasonal changes are not the result of being closer to or farther away from the sun; the difference between perihelion and aphelion is only about 3 percent—not enough to account for the differences we see in our seasons.

Another consequence of traveling in an elliptical orbit is that the earth must travel a longer distance from the beginning of spring to the beginning of autumn than it does from the beginning of autumn to the beginning of spring. (Skeptical? Count the days from March 21 to September 23 and compare to the number of days between September 23 to March 21.) Not only that, but the earth moves faster through its orbit when it is closer to the sun, from September to March, than when it is farther away, from March to September. For us in the northern hemisphere, it results in about a week-longer spring and summer than fall and winter. Still, these effects do not account for the change in seasons.

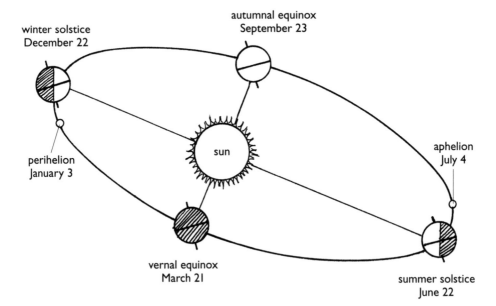

winter solstice
December 22

autumnal equinox
September 23

perihelion
January 3

sun

aphelion
July 4

vernal equinox
March 21

summer solstice
June 22

Earth Orbit in Perspective. March 21 (vernal equinox) and September 23 (autumnal equinox): Both hemispheres receive equal treatment from the sun: twelve hours from sunrise to sunset. Appearances are slightly deceiving, however: The atmosphere slightly bends the incoming light rays, so the sun can still be seen for a short while below the horizon, lengthening daylight a little past twelve hours.

June 22 (summer solstice): The northern hemisphere is tilted toward the sun; the North Pole receives 24-hour sunlight, the South Pole remains in daylong darkness. All points of the northern hemisphere receive more sunlight than do the corresponding parts of the southern hemisphere. At a latitude of 23.5° north of the equator, on the Tropic of Cancer, the sun appears directly overhead; the longest daylight of the year.

December 22 (winter solstice): It's the southern hemisphere's turn in the sun. The sun appears directly overhead at the Tropic of Capricorn, at 23.5° south latitude. The winter solstice brings the shortest daylight of the year for the northern hemisphere's start of winter.

FACT: The fall colors of deciduous leaves are primarily triggered by the shorter day length, not cooler temperatures.

Seasonal changes are the result of the earth's tilt of its axis with respect to its plane of orbit. In other words, the equator is not parallel to the orbital path. The angle of this tilt has varied over the past 100,000 years or so, but is now about 23.5 degrees. Because of this tilt, the axis points in the same direction into space (very close to the star Polaris) no matter what part of the orbit it is in, resulting in unequal heating of the earth's surface as it both rotates and revolves.

Because the atmosphere and the land and water surfaces of the earth take time to absorb heat, the warmest days lag behind the day of greatest sunshine. The warmest months over the continents are July and January, for the northern and southern hemispheres, respectively. Oceans are slower in absorbing and releasing heat, and in the northern hemisphere are coldest in March and warmest in September.

Heat received in the atmosphere creates changes and differences in air pressure, which in turn drives the winds on earth. The direction and speed of the winds, however, are the net result of other forces acting upon the moving air, including the *pressure gradient force* and *friction*. In addition, because the earth is a sphere twirling on its own axis underneath a loose wrapping of air, and we are observers from this same rotating reference system, several other effects on the wind are merely perceived from our vantage point and are considered apparent forces, including *centrifugal force* and the *Coriolis force*.

Centrifugal Force. The tendency of any moving object is to remain moving in a straight line unless another force acts upon it. The centrifugal force is that tendency of the air to keep moving in a straight, forward direction, which has the apparent effect of a force toward the outside of the axis of rotation. This is the force a rider in a car feels when a sudden left turn causes him to be jerked toward the right.

Coriolis Force. Another apparent force bends air and water currents toward the right in the northern hemisphere and to the left in the southern hemisphere. Called the Coriolis force, or Coriolis effect, after French mathematician Gaspard de Coriolis who first described it in 1835, it is not a real force, but only one that is perceived from our frame of reference on the spinning globe. Viewed against a non-moving framework, there is no effect.

Consider throwing a ball from the North Pole to the equator on a non-rotating earth. The ball's trajectory passes straight from pole to equator over a

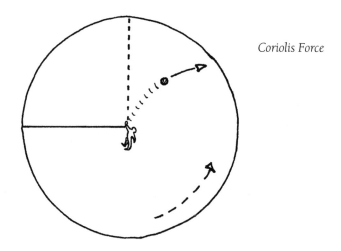

Coriolis Force

certain set of landmarks. Put the earth into motion, and throw the ball once again. Once again, the ball travels in a straight line to the equator, but because the earth is turning underneath the ball, its trajectory passes over a different set of landmarks to the right of its previous path, *appearing* to have been deflected to the right—the Coriolis effect. The longer the ball travels on its path, the more the earth rotates under it, and the farther it apparently deviates toward the right (west) of its straight way. Similarly, a ball—or air or water current—traveling northward from lower northern latitudes to higher will apparently be forced to the right of its direction of travel (or eastward).

Pressure Gradient Force. Much like a ball on the top of a hill is forced by gravity to the bottom of the hill, air flows from regions of higher pressure to those of lower pressure. This difference in pressure, called the pressure gradient, drives the winds, and works both horizontally and vertically. Vertically, the force is directed upward but is nearly balanced by gravity. Horizontally, the

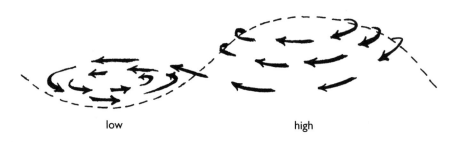

low   high

Wind Flow from High to Low Pressure Areas

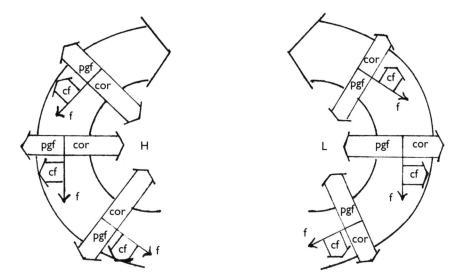

Sum of Forces Affecting Wind Direction around High and Low Pressure Areas

force acts from higher to lower pressure; the greater the pressure gradient, the faster the air moves, and hence the faster the wind speed.

Because of the Coriolis effect, air spreading out of the center of high pressure does not flow directly toward low pressure, but is deflected in a clockwise direction. As the air is drawn into a low pressure center, the wind spirals toward it in an opposite rotation, resulting in clockwise flow around a high and counterclockwise flow around a low. The opposite is true in the southern hemisphere.

Friction. Air moving near the surface is always influenced by the texture at the surface, and the resultant friction is obviously greater over rugged mountains than open water. The drag created by friction operates in the opposite direction to the air movement and reduces its speed, which in turn reduces the effect of the Coriolis force on the direction of the wind. The effect of friction is important only in the lower 5,000 feet of the atmosphere.

> FACT: On sunny, windy days, young spiderlings climb to an elevated position and begin spinning silk. As the thread lengthens to several feet, it is picked up by the wind, with the spiderling still attached for the ride of its life, in a weather-generated dispersal of the newest generation.

OBSERVATIONS AND ACTIVITIES

The Old Tumbler Trick. Here's a surprising way to observe air pressure without the use of measuring instruments.

Materials: Drinking cup, index card, water.

To Know: Atmospheric pressure is exerted by the density of the gases in the air, and is not dependent on the orientation of the surface upon which it acts. The surface can even be upside down, as this activity so forcefully demonstrates.

To Do: Fill the drinking cup to the brim with water. Place the index card on top of the cup's rim, making sure it covers the entire surface of the rim. Pick up the cup and carefully turn it upside down. The air pressure outside the cup—greater than the water pressure inside the cup—holds the water in its place.

Make a Water Barometer. Measure changes in atmospheric pressure with a simple barometer.

Materials: Plastic water bottle with screw-on lid and straw, small piece of plasticene clay, shallow bowl, water, food coloring, index card, masking tape, paper clip, pliers.

To Know: The force exerted by the atmosphere on the surface of the earth varies with the amount of air above it. More air above means higher pressure at the surface; less air means less pressure. A barometer reacts to the weight of the air above it and detects changes in pressure, which are associated with changes in the weather.

To Do: Tightly screw the lid onto the bottle, with the straw extended about 8 inches. Use a small bit of clay to seal the lid around the straw to make it completely airtight. Put some water in the shallow bowl and add a little food coloring. Turn the bottle upside down and insert the tip of the straw into the water. Slightly squeeze the bottle until a few bubbles rise through the water, and the water rises about halfway up the straw. Tape the water bottle to an inside corner to hold it in place.

Fold the index card in half lengthwise and tape it to the back of the straw. Use the pliers to squeeze the longer loop of the paper clip into a sharper angle to use as a pointer, and clip it to the card to mark the height of the water column in the straw. Compare the change in height of the water in the tube every day. How does it correlate to the weather?

Earth-o-meter. With this homemade gadget, you can measure the speed of earth's rotation and compute the length of the day.

Materials: Magnifying lens, piece of cardboard, pencil, stool or chair, masking tape, wristwatch, sunny day.

To Know: The earth makes one complete rotation on its axis per day. This is what makes the sun appear to move across the sky.

To Do: Pick a sunny location outside, and tape the handle of the magnifying lens on the chair so that the lens extends horizontally over the edge of the seat. Place the cardboard where the sun shines through the lens toward the ground. Raise the chair or the paper until a focused image of the sun appears on the cardboard and prop them in place. Trace the focused image on the paper with the pencil. Measure the time in seconds it takes for the image to entirely leave the circle you've drawn.

Because the sun's diameter in the sky is approximately one half of 1 degree, in the amount of time it takes for its image to move out of the circle, the earth has rotated one half of 1 degree of its 360-degree rotation. Multiply your time by 720 to calculate the length of earth's day, in seconds. How close did you come to the solar day of 86,400 seconds? You can convert the seconds to minutes, then the minutes to hours, to see how close you came to the normal day of 24 hours.

CHAPTER 2

Sun:
All Systems 'Go'

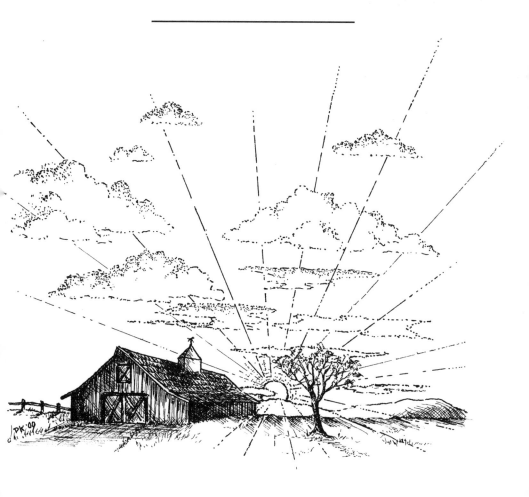

The real mixer at the weather party is heat. Without it, things would really be dull—in fact, dead. But fortunately, the sun is a real gas, constantly bathing earth in radiation. Heat from this radiation stirs the atmosphere into action, creating an environment in which all weather systems are "go."

Radiation is simply the transfer of energy that comes by the rapid oscillations of an electromagnetic field in space. Radiation can be visualized as a traveling wave, with a certain wavelength, frequency, and speed. Sunlight, radio waves, TV waves, microwaves, and X rays are all basically the same thing: electromagnetic waves transmitting energy. They all travel at the same speed as light, but their differences are in their wavelengths and frequencies.

Heat energy supplied by the sun's radiation is called *insolation.* The term comes from the words *in*coming *sol*ar radi*ation,* and must not be confused with insulation, referring to materials that do not readily conduct heat or electricity. As the insolation streaks toward the earth, its passage is challenged by the atmosphere. Part of the insolation is reflected back to space, part is scattered or absorbed by the air, and part reaches the ground.

The size and properties of gas molecules in the atmosphere determine the amount of scattering and absorption. Ozone is the most effective absorber of radiation, capturing nearly all of the ultraviolet (short) wavelengths. Scattering is the reason for the brightness of the sky, distributing energy in all directions, and is also the explanation behind the colors of the sunset and why the sky is blue.

Despite the steadiness of the sun's output, the rate of insolation at the earth's surface varies a great deal. Different rates occur as the angle at which the sun's rays strike the surface changes, both daily and seasonally. The distance from the sun to the earth and the amount of radiation absorbed by the atmosphere also affect the amount of insolation. More radiation reaches the surface on clear days than on cloudy ones; in fact, very dense cloud formations may block as much as 90 percent of the insolation.

Insolation at the earth's equator is greater than anywhere else on the surface because the sun's rays are more perpendicular there more of the year than anywhere else. More radiation per equal area (and therefore more heat) reaches the equatorial zone than the temperate zones, where incoming rays are more slanted.

Overall, the atmosphere loses heat while the earth's surface, except near the poles, gains it. In order to keep the tropics from continually getting warmer and the poles from continually getting colder, energy is transferred from lower to higher latitudes. This horizontal heat exchange is conducted primarily through atmospheric circulations, ocean currents, and the release of latent heat through condensation of moisture carried poleward.

Still, if there were not a continual dispersal and loss of the heat from the continual incoming solar radiation, things would get awfully warm. (This incoming radiation consists of shortwave energy in the ultraviolet, visible, and near-infrared wavelengths of light.) Fortunately the earth radiates heat back into the atmosphere in the form of longwave energy (consisting of thermal infrared wavelengths) known as *terrestrial radiation*. The net outgoing radiation, on the average, balances the net incoming radiation, with the happy result that we neither freeze nor fry.

As terrestrial radiation leaves the earth, impurities in the air absorb a considerable amount of this heat. Water vapor in the air also absorbs some of the outgoing radiation. A humid atmosphere, even on a clear night, absorbs quite a bit of this heat and greatly restricts the amount of nighttime cooling. But a clear night with a dry atmosphere allows a lot of heat to escape to space.

The various surfaces and objects of the earth absorb the incoming shortwave radiation from the sun and warm. Generally, land is a better absorber of the incoming shortwave radiation than water, which in turn is a better absorber than the air. Also, the coarser and darker an object is, the less radiation it reflects and the more it absorbs. The more insolation an object can absorb, the slower it heats up, but the longer it stays warm.

Consider the following natural occurrences casually but routinely observed: The air around us heats up and then cools drastically in one 24-hour period; the ocean water temperature, though cool in May, is nice and warm in September; barn cellars of stone and mortar construction and shielded with earth remain practically the same temperature year-round, along with the interior of caves. The rocks and soil of the earth's crust are actually the very best natural absorbers of insolation.

FACT: The sun produces more energy in one second than we have produced in all of human history.

The radiation reflectivity of an object is called *albedo,* and ranges from a perfectly black object with a value of 0, to a perfectly white diffuse reflector with a value of 1, or 100 percent. What isn't reflected is absorbed, and heats the object. This is commonly illustrated by the dark-colored paved surface of a road or parking lot that melts away a covering of snow long before the lighter-

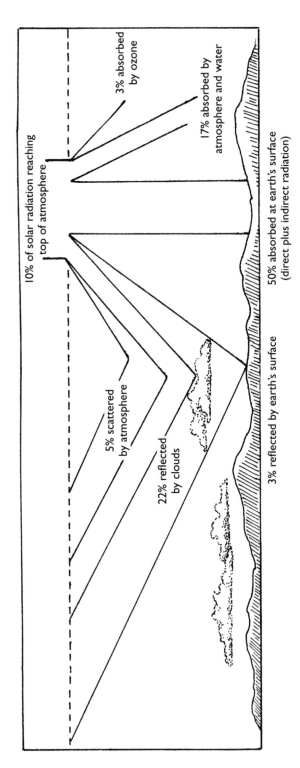

Solar Radiation Balance of Earth and Atmosphere

10% of solar radiation reaching top of atmosphere

3% absorbed by ozone

17% absorbed by atmosphere and water

50% absorbed at earth's surface (direct plus indirect radiation)

5% scattered by atmosphere

22% reflected by clouds

3% reflected by earth's surface

colored ground or grassy surfaces do. Cloud albedo varies greatly depending on cloud thickness, cloud droplet size, air pollution, and whether the cloud is composed of droplets or crystals. The overall albedo of the earth has been determined by extensive satellite measurements to be close to .3, or 30 percent. This means the earth reflects 30 percent of radiation and absorbs 70 percent.

TYPICAL RADIATION REFLECTIVITY (ALBEDO) OF TERRESTRIAL SURFACES

Surface	% of Radiation Reflected*
Water (sun high in sky)	2-10
Water (sun near horizon)	90
Forests	8-15
Cultivated areas	10-20
Bare soil, sand, rock	10-30
Old snow, sea ice	50-60
Fresh snow	70-80
Thin cloud	10-30
Thick cloud	70-90

*What isn't reflected is absorbed.

GLOBAL CIRCULATIONS

More energy is received from the sun in the tropical and subtropical regions than is radiated back into space. Because of the difference in heating between poles and equator, heat is continually being transferred from lower to higher latitudes—from the equatorial region toward the poles.

Because heating is greatest at the equator, the air there tends to rise and expand to a greater extent than anywhere else. As the equatorial air rises, moisture-laden air at low altitudes and from higher latitudes in both hemispheres moves toward the equator to take its place and meets in a turbulent tumble called the *intertropical convergence zone*. This band of active weather is characterized by strong upward heat flow, heavy thunderstorm precipitation, and low surface pressure. The flow toward the equator at the surface is balanced by a flow away from the equator at higher altitudes.

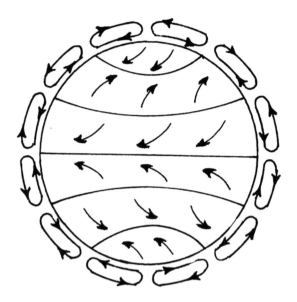

Simplified Global Air Circulation Patterns

Where the upper-level air descends at about 30° north and south, surface weather is characterized by high pressure, with the fair skies and calm of the *horse latitudes*. Here, the pressure gradient and the Coriolis force work together to direct a portion of this descending flow back toward the equator, creating the northeast trade winds of the northern hemisphere and the southeast trades of the southern hemisphere. The resultant vertical circulating cell reaches as high as 12 miles, with an overall speed of about 5 mph.

At midlatitudes, surface winds flow as the prevailing westerlies of both hemispheres, while another vertical circulating cell rises at about 50° north and south to also descend in the horse latitudes. Weak polar cells also circulate in the upper levels of the far north and south.

LOCAL AND REGIONAL CIRCULATIONS

On a small scale, irregularities in terrain and uneven heating or cooling of the surface are always producing local variations in the global flow of air.

Free Convection. Whenever the air is locally heated to a point where it is warmer than the surrounding air, *free convection* occurs: The parcel of air becomes buoyant and begins to rise, much like a hot air balloon. Without any other sources or losses of heat present, the temperature of the rising parcel decreases at a steady rate of 5.4°F per 1,000 feet of altitude. As the parcel rises, the pressure about it decreases, and buoyant air expands and cools.

THE GREENHOUSE EFFECT

Part of the earth's terrestrial longwave, or infrared, radiation is absorbed by carbon dioxide, water vapor, and methane (the so-called greenhouse gases of the atmosphere) and is then reradiated back to earth. This heat is trapped, or recycled, completely inside the earth's system, and brings the average global temperature to a life-friendly 59°F, some 80 to 100°F warmer than it otherwise would be.

This behavior is called the greenhouse effect, because of its similarity (or so it was thought) to how the interior of a greenhouse heats up. Glass of the greenhouse, so the theory went, allows shortwave radiation from the sun to pass through. At the same time, the theory said, the glass blocks the longwave radiation being emitted from the warmed objects inside, trapping that heat inside the greenhouse.

However it's since been proven that that's not the real reason a greenhouse is a hothouse. Instead, the glass simply prohibits the inside, warmer air from mixing with the outside, cooler air.

So the earth stays warmer by the greenhouse effect—receiving shortwave sunlight through the atmosphere, absorbing it, and radiating thermal longwave radiation that becomes trapped within the atmosphere—while a real greenhouse does not.

As long as this air remains warmer than its surroundings, it will continue to rise and continue to transfer heat from lower regions to upper levels. But if the rate of decrease in the surrounding air is less than 5.4°F per 1,000 feet, the rising parcel will eventually become cooler than its surroundings and sink back to its original level, warming in the increasing pressure of lower altitude.

But if the temperature of the environment decreases with height faster than 5.4°F/1,000 ft., the rising parcel of air will remain warmer than its surroundings, and will continue to rise and accelerate away from its original level, in a condition called *instability*. If the rising air is sufficiently moist, cumulus clouds may form, but the latent heat of condensation released into the parcel slows its cooling to the wet adiabatic lapse rate of 3°F/1,000 ft., thereby increasing the temperature difference between itself and its surroundings, and increasing its buoyancy and instability.

Free convection may be thought of as "warm air rises," although more correctly, you may want to remember that "light air rises." In the presence of water

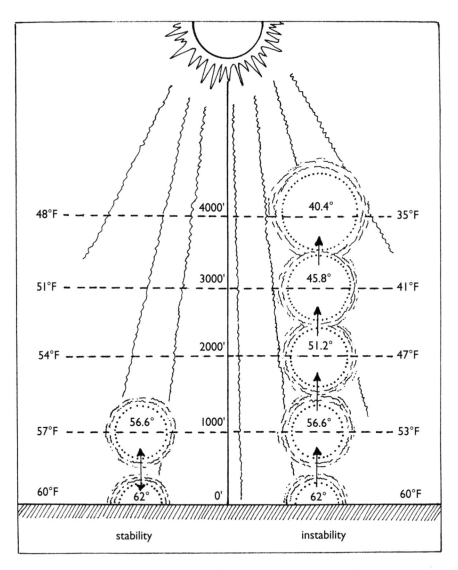

48°F		4000'	40.4°	35°F
51°F		3000'	45.8°	41°F
54°F		2000'	51.2°	47°F
57°F	56.6°	1000'	56.6°	53°F
60°F	62°	0'	62°	60°F

stability   instability

Stability and Instability. *A parcel of air slightly warmed by the sun will rise, expand, and cool at the dry adiabatic lapse rate of 5.4°F per thousand feet.*

Stability. *If the parcel of air becomes cooler than its surroundings, it will sink back to its original level and warm.*

Instability. *If the parcel of air remains warmer than its surroundings, it will continue to rise until it reaches the same temperature as its surroundings.*

vapor—which weighs much less than either oxygen or nitrogen, which together make up 99 percent of the air—free convection is all the more favorable.

In coastal areas, the water temperature changes little over a twenty-four-hour period compared with the temperature of the adjacent land. This variation may result in a land temperature much warmer than the water by day and much cooler than the water by night. Warmer air will rise, of course, no matter what surface it is over, and the resultant flow sets up a localized circulation.

As warm air rises over the land during the day, the cooler air flows toward the land to replace it in what is called a *sea breeze*. At night, cooler air over the land flows seaward to replace the warmer air rising over the water, resulting in a *land breeze*. Sea breezes rarely generate much precipitation, but can often produce fog when the moist, warm air moving onshore meets cooler air inland and condenses.

FACT: Inside each broadleaf, millions of green-colored chloroplasts use radiant energy from the sun to convert carbon dioxide and water into glucose, a food for the plant.

A similar daily circulation occurs farther inland, where the differences in heating of mountains and valleys produce breezes. As the morning sun heats the valley floor, buoyant air rises upslope, creating a *valley breeze,* which tends to last from midmorning to sunset. With the loss of the sun, the air loses its heat and its buoyancy, and a *mountain breeze* brings heavier, cooler air downslope to the valley, usually from after midnight until just after sunrise—when the circulation again reverses itself.

Forced Lifting and Sinking. The forced lifting and sinking of air *(forced convection)* occurs when air is forced upward or downward without first being warmed or cooled. This happens in nature in several different ways. Air flowing along upsloping terrain is known as *orographic lifting.* When air is lifted by rising over cooler air, it is called *overrunning.* Cooler air advancing against warmer air sinks, producing the opposite of overrunning, called *downslope motion.* Air also is forced aloft by being caught up in the rising and sinking motions associated with atmospheric highs and lows.

Mountainous regions, simply by their unique topography, may at times funnel cool air from a high plateau downslope into the valleys. This may be a gentle but cold breeze. But where the air passes over snow and ice and loses heat rapidly, then drains into narrow, V-shaped valleys, the wind can become quite strong. These distinctive mountain winds usually earn their own local names, such as the *mistral* of the Alps that pours its way to the French coast of the Mediterranean.

A different effect is produced as moist air flows over a mountain. As moist air rises, it cools with height at a rate of 3°F per 1,000 feet (not nearly as fast as the dry-air rate of 5.4°F per 1,000 feet). Eventually clouds develop, and precipitation wrings moisture from the air. At the summit, the air is now both warmer and drier than air of the same altitude that has not climbed the mountain. But as the air passes over the summit and flows down the other side of the mountain, it compresses and warms at 5.4°F per 1,000 feet (now following the dry-air rate), creating a much warmer, dryer wind. That means a rise in temperature of 33°F for a drop in elevation of 6,000 feet.

Such a dry wind evaporates and sublimates moisture from everything it passes over, melting snowpacks, drying forests, desiccating wooden structures, and creating fire hazards, as well as generating irritability in humans. On the lee side of the Rocky Mountains, the strong and gusty warm wind is called the Chinook, named after the Chinook Indians of the northern Rockies, and means "snow eater." With relative humidities of 40 percent or less, and the ability to raise the temperature at the bottom of a slope as much as 50°F in a few hours, a lusty Chinook can gobble up to two feet of snow in as little as twenty-four hours. A Chinook that bit into Havre, Montana, once raised the temperature from 11°F to 42°F in less than three minutes.

Chinook winds are characteristic of nearly all mountain ranges throughout the world. In California—where the wind originates in the high plateau of Nevada, blows fiercely through Santa Ana Canyon, and brings heat and fine dust all the way to Los Angeles—it is known as the Santa Ana wind. In the Alps, it's called the *foehn*, in Argentina, it's the *zonda,* and in the Andes, it's the *puelche.* This wind is known in France as the *aspre,* and in Majorca as the *sky sweeper.* In the New Zealand Alps, the wind is a *Canterbury northwester.*

Convergence and Divergence. Regional circulations also are caused by the fluid nature of the atmosphere itself. Because of the law of conservation of mass, the only way the total amount of air in a given volume can decrease is by having more air flow out than what flows in. When air is heated, strong upper-level winds transport the rising air completely out of the region. Air leaving like this—called *divergence*—sets up a vertical motion much as the draft up a chimney. With air leaving vertically, there must also be air arriving at the surface to take its place—called *convergence.*

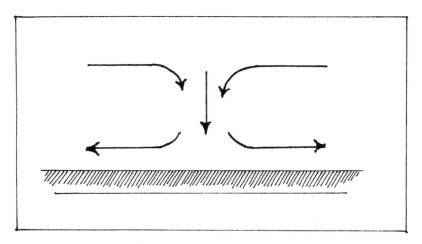

Upper-level Convergence. *Upper-level convergence produces sinking motion in the mid-levels, and divergence and rising pressure at the lower level.*

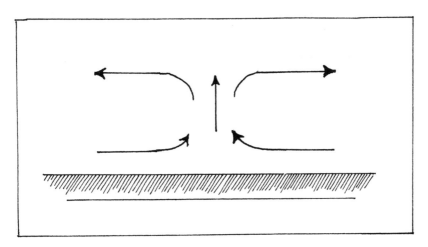

Upper-level Divergence. *Upper-level divergence produces upward motion in the mid-levels, and convergence and falling pressure at the lower level.*

The relationship between the two behaviors is pretty simple: If there is horizontal divergence at upper levels of the atmosphere, there must be convergence at the lower levels, and vice versa. Convergence and divergence are directly related to the formation and intensification of *cyclones* (low pressure areas) and *anticyclones* (high pressure areas). The same vertical motion that produces precipitation in a cyclone also causes the storm to intensify. When this happens, the divergence aloft is slightly stronger than the convergence near the ground, and the resulting net loss of air is measured by falling pressure at the surface. If the low-level convergence is stronger some distance away from the low pressure center, the surface cyclone is likely heading in that direction. Meanwhile, low-level divergence (and upper-level convergence) is associated with the high pressure centers that follow cyclones.

CYCLONES

A cyclone is a storm system that rotates about a center of low pressure. Midlatitude cyclones typically get their start near the transition zones between warm and cold air masses. (See chapter 6 for a full discussion of tropical cyclones, hurricanes, and the snowstorms caused by midlatitude cyclones.) Because the air is fluid in nature, two adjacent masses will not keep to themselves as if cooped up in a room with walls. The adjoining edges begin to mix; as they do, the heavier, colder air displaces the lighter, warmer air at the surface, which rises over the colder.

When this happens, the pressure at the surface decreases because lighter air has replaced a portion of the heavier air in the upper levels, resulting in a lighter column of air above the surface. As other surface-level air converges toward the lower pressure, the Coriolis force deflects it, and convergence is channeled into narrow bands as the wind begins a counterclockwise rotation around the developing cyclone. With convergence at the lower levels, the newly arriving air rises upward to diverge at the upper levels, and intensification of the low pressure begins.

The narrow bands of low-level convergence that form between two differing air masses are known as weather fronts. As these fronts move and modulate, the cyclone intensifies, advances and matures, stirring the differences in

Life Cycle of a Cyclone

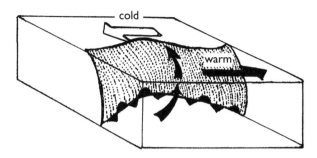

a. The initial meeting of air masses creates instability that leads to a deformation in their leading edges.

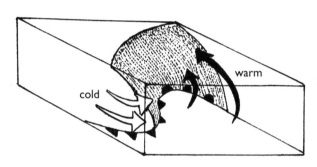

b. The deformation, in turn, leads to an eastward advance of the cold air to the south, a westward retreat of the cold air to the north, and the formation of a warm sector. Simultaneously, the pressure decreases at the apex of the developing wave, and a low pressure center forms, called a cyclone.

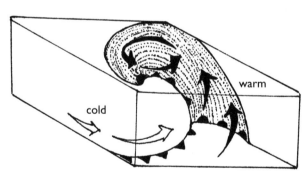

c. The cyclone intensifies as the cold air advances until it overtakes the retreating wedge of warm air. With the low pressure completely cut off from the warm air, convergence at the surface ceases. The low may be a rather intense system by this time, but the action at the surface is over; the formerly warm air mass swirls aloft, having cooled in the lifting process.

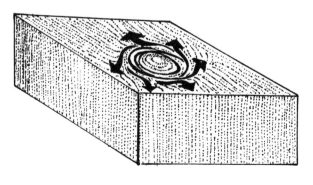

d. The contrasts between air masses is no longer significant, friction at the surface weakens the flow, and the cyclone dissolves.

wind, water, heat, and pressure of the air masses to a more homogenous mix before eventually dissolving.

Taken together, the convergence, divergence, vertical motions, and weather fronts develop a characteristic shape in midlatitude cyclones, easily seen in the satellite images of a comma-shaped cloud cover. The largest mass of clouds over and ahead of the low pressure center indicates the region of strongest upper-level divergence, carrying away the air that had ascended ahead of the cyclone and along the warm front.

Extending southward from the cyclone is the cloud-comma's tail, indicative of clouds associated with the cold front. In a well-developed but dying storm, a spiraling of the clouds can be seen about the cyclone's center, as the comma head moves downstream away from the cyclone, and the spin of the storm wraps itself in bands of clouds.

SURFACE FRONTAL WEATHER

The passage of a weather front does not bring about an instantaneous change in conditions, since the front itself is not a sharply defined boundary between two air masses. It is, rather, a zone of rapid transition in temperature, humidity, pressure, and wind direction between the air masses.

Each kind of front produces characteristic weather. Cooler air advancing against retreating warmer air is a *cold front*. Warmer air overrunning cooler, slower-moving air is *warm front*. A front is a *stationary front* if little movement is occurring in any direction between the air masses. In an *occluded front*, an advancing cold front overtakes an advancing warm front at the surface.

Cold Front. Ahead of a cold front, the air is relatively warm and humid. Winds are generally from the south or southwest, gradually getting stronger. Barometric pressure falls, and showers or thunderstorms may be present. The leading edge of the cold front, which usually moves southward or eastward, brings with it a noticeable change in wind direction, now from the west or northwest.

The temperature begins to fall with the shift in the winds, or soon after. Precipitation is normally associated with frontal passage and may last a few hours. The most rapid temperature drop and the strongest winds are also associated with the frontal zone, both gradually diminishing with time. After frontal passage, barometric pressure begins to rise and precipitation gives way to clearing and drier skies.

Conditions are sometimes favorable for the formation of lines of thunderstorms—*squall lines*—in a band ahead of a fast-moving cold front and extend-

SYMBOLS:
SURFACE FRONTAL SYSTEMS

▲▲▲▲▲	●●●●●
cold front	warm front
●▼●▼●	▲●▲●▲
stationary front	occluded front
— — — — —	——··——··——··
trough	squall line
△△△△△	⌒⌒⌒⌒⌒
cold front aloft	warm front aloft
L	**H**
low pressure center	high pressure center

ing into the warm sector. These intense storms approach quickly and look like a nasty, roiling, black wall of cloud. They occur when winds above the cold front, moving in the same direction as the front itself, slam into the warm air mass. Not much stormy weather actually occurs at the frontal boundary in this case, but 100 to 150 miles ahead of the front, the strong winds explosively force warmer air upward, producing the extremely turbulent squall line. The continual formation of squall lines can have devastating effects, as they had in the severe flooding of the Midwest in the summer of 1993.

Warm Front. The passage of a warm front at the surface is presaged by increasing and lowering clouds. The overrunning of warmer air on top of cooler air brings cooling that results in condensation and extensive clouds. Because the warm front slopes upward over the cooler air, both the clouds and precipitation associated with the front occur well in advance of it.

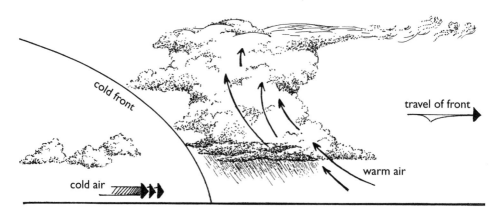

Cold Front. *A cold front is the leading edge of a colder air mass that is replacing warmer air at the surface. Cold fronts range in length from a few hundred to a few thousand miles and can last from a day or so to a week or more. The ratio of height to distance (vertical slope) is typically about 1 to 50, but varies considerably from situation to situation.*

Characteristic cloud patterns tend to be layered clouds because of the stability of the atmosphere (warm over cool air). The typical warm-front cloud sequence starts with the highest cirrus and cirrostratus well ahead of the front, lowering to altostratus or altocumulus, then to stratocumulus, and finally to the lowest nimbostratus, stratus, or cumulonimbus at the surface

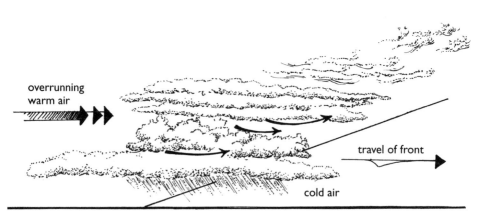

Warm Front. *A warm front is the zone of rapid transition between advancing warmer air and retreating colder air at the surface, dragged into a wedge by friction with the ground. Because the warm front rises over the retreating cold air, the associated clouds and precipitation occur ahead of the frontal boundary at the surface, and range from several hundred to a thousand miles. The ratio of height to distance (vertical slope) is much less than the cold front, typically between 1 to 100 and 1 to 150.*

frontal zone.(See chapter 4, on clouds.) This cloud sequence may stretch for several hundred to more than a thousand miles in front of the surface front.

Warm-front precipitation is normally shed over an extensive area. It may extend through the full parade of clouds, with the lightest precipitation from the highest clouds not even reaching the ground, and a lingering soaking from the thick cloud cover at the front. Following passage of the warm front, the pressure falls, but temperature rises; the surface wind, which may be weak and variable before the passage, usually shifts to come out of the south or southwest. The changes associated with a warm front are usually less intense than those accompanying a cold front.

Occluded Front. An occluded front forms when an advancing cold front overtakes an advancing warm front at the surface. The occluded front can be described as a "back to back" front whose formation involves three distinct air masses in two possible scenarios.

When the overtaking air is colder than the cool air wedging out in front of the warm front, the cold air pushes under both the warm air and the cool air, and the warm air is lifted entirely off the surface. Because the advancing air is colder than the air it is replacing, the effect is very similar to a cold front, and the result is known as a *cold-type occluded front.*

When the overtaking cool air is warmer than the retreating air in front of the warm front, the advancing cool air rises over the colder air mass and produces weather similar to that of warm fronts. This *warm-type occluded front*

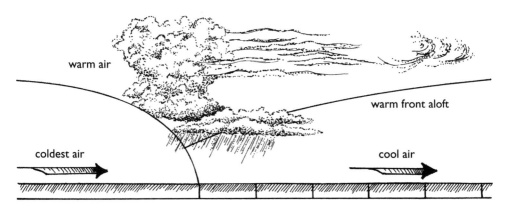

Cold-type Occluded Front. *A cold occlusion occurs as advancing cold air meets cool air at the surface. The warmest air is forced aloft; its boundary with the cold air is usually west of the surface front.*

WIND SHEAR

Whenever wind varies in either speed or direction over relatively short horizontal or vertical distances, it causes shearing stresses in the moving air. Faster air tends to pull the slower air along toward its direction. The difference between these winds over this distance is called the *wind shear.*

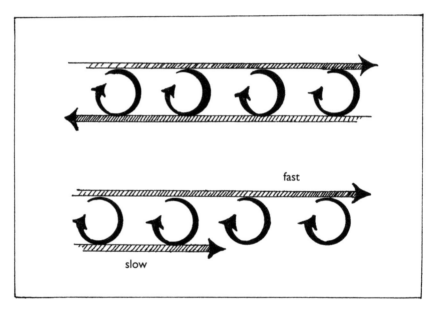

fast

slow

Wind Shear. *Wind blowing in different directions between adjacent layers causes turbulent eddies to form between them. The same effect occurs when the wind speeds differ, even though their directions are the same.*

occurs occasionally in the western United States when the westerly flow behind a Pacific cold front is not as cold as the air over the continent.

Weather produced ahead of an occluded front is similar to that ahead of a warm front, and that which follows it is similar to the weather after a cold front. High clouds stretch out a few hundred miles in advance of the front,

Differences in wind direction or changes in speed over a short distance create eddies in the air that cause turbulence, which can be quite treacherous to air travelers. One type of shear, called *microbursts*, forms in the cold air that blasts downward out of severe thunderstorms. Another kind, *clear air turbulence*, occurs without any sign of clouds and presents hazards to high-flying aircraft as they approach the jet stream.

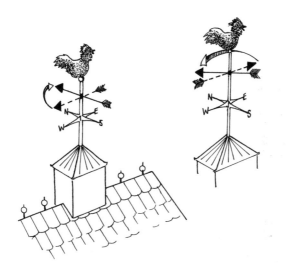

Backing and Veering Wind. *If wind changes with height, or with length, in a counterclockwise direction, the wind is said to be* backing. *If the change in direction is clockwise, it is called* veering. *Simply noting this kind of change over time will give you quite a reliable short-range forecast, summed up in an old saying:*

> *A veering wind, fair weather;*
> *A backing wind, foul weather.*
> *If wind follows sun's course, expect fair weather.*

lowering and thickening closer to the front at the surface. Persistent, heavy rain is often wrung out of the elevated warm air and at the zone directly in advance of the surface front.

Once this passes, drier and clearer air follows, but temperatures at the surface remain nearly constant, with perhaps a slight maximum during frontal

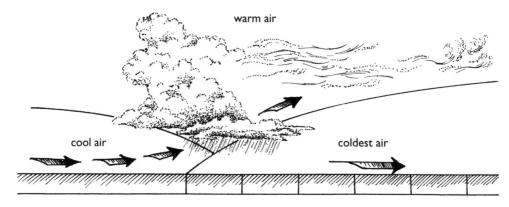

Warm-type Occluded Front. *A warm occlusion occurs when advancing cool air over-takes retreating colder air at the surface. The cool air rides over the colder air; their boundary is usually east of the surface front.*

passage. Wind direction normally shifts from an easterly or southerly direction before the front to a westerly or northerly course afterward.

UPPER AIR MOVEMENTS

Storm development is obviously not confined to frontal zones and to weather at the surface, but extends upward through the troposphere. Air streams at all levels add their influences to the storm process. These streams can be thought of as conveyor belts that transport volumes of air throughout the depth and breadth of the system.

In upper levels, strong narrow currents of air known as *jet streams* extend for hundreds or even thousands of miles across the hemisphere. They generally occur in the overlapping tropopause at 30° and 60° north and south, respectively identified as the subtropical and polar jets.

These tubular transports of high-speed air powerfully influence the scope, direction, and life of surface cyclones and anticyclones as they shift and meander north and south. Closely tied to the temperature gradients across weather fronts, the jet streams are the primary channels for both horizontal and vertical mixing of air. As these undulating streams work their way eastward (in the northern hemisphere), they scout out the future direction of a storm. While the forward speed of a cyclone is typically 20 to 30 mph, the air traveling within the core of the jet stream often exceeds 150 mph.

Often found in the immediate vicinity of a storm, especially one rapidly intensifying, are narrow, high-velocity air streams called *jet streaks*. These are

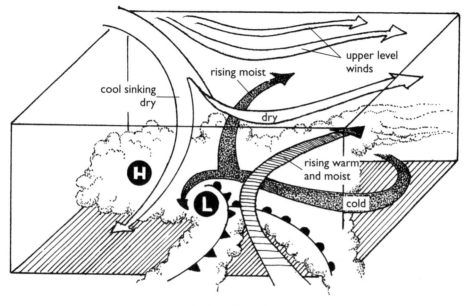

Cyclone Conveyors

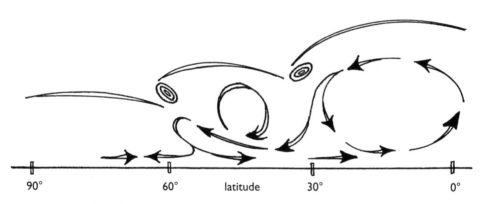

90°	60°	30°	0°
		latitude	

Jet Streams (Northern Hemisphere)*. Because temperature does not decrease uniformly with height with respect to latitude, pressure decreases more rapidly with height to the north than to the south, creating a height difference in the tropopause. Jet streams form in these discontinuities of the tropopause where the pressure gradient—and hence the wind—is strongest.*

Generally the polar jet stream is stronger in the winter, when north-south temperature differences are the greatest, and it may circle the globe in a continuous flow. The polar jet averages about 6.5 miles high flowing at 134 mph, but it can reach speeds twice that fast in winter.

The subtropical jet stream is found at an altitude of about 8 miles with a average speed of 90 mph. The transition zone between warmer air to the south and colder air to the north is called the polar front. Arrows show general circulatory flow.

regions of accelerated winds associated with the jet stream and may occur in the upper troposphere near the jet stream, or in the lower troposphere, only slightly above a surface cyclone. With strong upper-level divergence over a surface cyclone, air is vigorously pumped upward in the jet streak, decreasing pressure at the surface and increasing the development of the storm and precipitation.

Upper-level Troughs and Ridges. Most people are familiar with topographic maps, and with the fact that contour lines on them represent equal elevations above sea level. It is very easy to identify hills and valleys on such a map. In a similar way, meteorologists use maps to indicate certain levels in the atmosphere, and they talk about the hills and valleys—the ridges and troughs—of that environment.

One such map is called the 500 millibar surface, in which the atmosphere is plotted with respect to pressure. (The 500 mb level is at the approximate midpoint of the atmosphere, with about half of the air below that level and half above it, varying in altitude from about 16,000 to 19,000 feet.) Contours are used to show lines of altitude of the constant 500 mb pressure level. The valleys, or troughs, show where the 500 mb surface is closer to the ground (with lower pressure at a constant height surface); the hills, or ridges, show where 500 mb is farther from the ground (with higher pressure at a constant height).

An interesting thing about troughs and ridges is how the winds respond to them. On the ground, a river will flow through the center, or lowest part, of a valley. But the air, being even more fluid than water, is not so forcefully directed. Instead of flowing through the lowest part of the trough, the air-

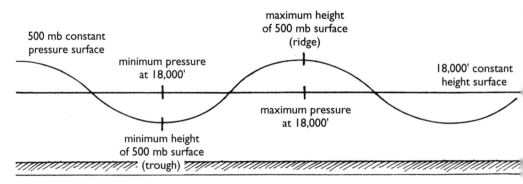

Ridge and Trough in the Constant Pressure Surface

DISCOVER NATURE IN THE WEATHER

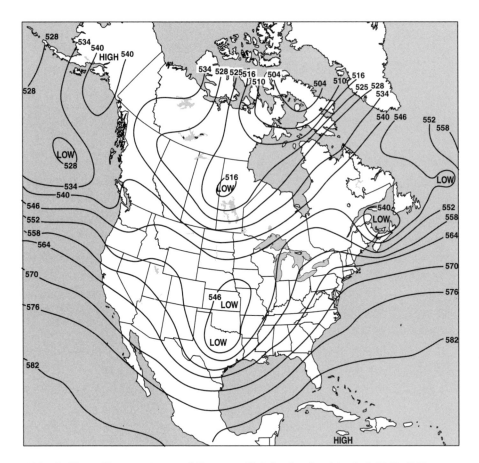

500 mb Chart Showing Lines of Constant Height. *Sunday, March 8, 1998, 7:00 A.M. EST. Compare the analysis of this level to the surface map for this same date, shown on page 179.*

Lines of equal values are often plotted on a weather map to enhance analysis. Generally speaking, these lines are called isolines. *This chart shows* isoheights, *lines of constant height.*

stream skirts counterclockwise about its edges, forming a U shape. Similarly, the air flows clockwise around a ridge in an inverted U. On a map, it is easy to depict this flow as a wave, with its associated trough and ridge.

These ridges and troughs in the pressure surfaces of the upper air are not necessarily found directly above surface-level highs and lows, although they do influence each other. The weather features of the surface tend to be steered by upper-level streams that eddy around the troughs and ridges.

FACT: The world's highest measured surface wind gust was recorded on April 12, 1934, at the summit of Mount Washington, in New Hampshire: 231 mph.

OBSERVATIONS AND ACTIVITIES

Taking the Heat. Here's a way for you to figure out the rates of heat absorbed and retained by an object.

The rates depend on the relationship between the distance and angle of a heat source, coupled with the object's basic characteristics.

Materials: Neck lamp with 100-watt bulb, five thermometers, 1-meter stick or yardstick, tape, timer, pencil, graph paper, paper cups, water, soil.

To Know: The earth's curved surface receives solar radiation at unequal angles and intensities, leading to the circulations of the wind. Land and water surfaces absorb and lose heat at slower rates than the air does.

To Do: Tape the thermometers across the meter stick at 0, 25, 50, 75, and 100 cm. (You could also use a yardstick, with the thermometers at 0, 9, 18, 27, and 36 inches.) Do not cover the thermometer bulbs. Lay the stick on a table, with the zero end next to the lamp, adjust the neck of the lamp to point the light bulb at the thermometer taped at 0, and turn on the lamp. Record the temperatures of each of the five thermometers at 1-minute intervals for 10 minutes. Turn off the lamp, and record the temperatures of each at 1-minute intervals as they cool for 10 minutes. Graph the temperatures of each thermometer versus time. How do the results relate to the climates of different latitudes? of the hemisphere's seasons?

Repeat the experiment with the thermometer bulbs in cups of water at these same distances, then in cups of soil. Extend the heating and cooling periods to 20 minutes each, reading the temperatures every 2 minutes. How do these results compare with the heating and cooling of the air?

Create an Inversion. This striking demonstration shows how a temperature inversion can prevent vertical movements of air.

Materials: Aquarium tank, ice cubes, neck lamp with 100-watt bulb, plastic wrap or glass cover, incense, matches.

To Know: A temperature inversion is a condition in which temperature increases with height, and is basically stable. A layer of warm air over cold air acts as a lid to confine movement and mixing to the layer below. Lingering inversions over cities surrounded by mountains prevent pollutants from rising and dissipating in the wind, and can lead to smog.

To Do: Place several ice cubes on the bottom of the aquarium. Turn on the lamp and point it into the aquarium. Wait four to five minutes.

Now light a piece of incense and blow it out so it smolders and produces smoke; place it in the center of the aquarium bottom. Cover the aquarium top completely with plastic wrap or a piece of glass.

Observe where the smoke layer settles. With the warm air at the top of the aquarium, representing a temperature inversion, the smoke is trapped below.

Booking Frontal Passage. Record the approach and passing of a weather front. Your TV weathercaster will let you know when a front is due on your doorstep. Make hourly observations of temperature, pressure, wind direction, clouds, and precipitation types and amounts. Does the temperature rise or fall? Does the wind back or veer? How can you tell when the front has passed?

Forever Blowing Bubbles. Blow soap bubbles to track low-altitude winds. Release them from various heights, over various surfaces (grass, dark pavement, etc.), and in various places.

How does the wind pattern differ near a building from out in the open? How does it differ in the woods from in a field?

Blow large bubbles in very cold air and observe their surfaces for the growth of ice crystals. Cool some of the solution in the refrigerator for a few minutes; warm some more on the stove. Blow hot and cold bubbles. How do they act and travel differently? Assure your friends it's research.

CHAPTER 3

Water:
What Goes
Around . . .

Water, the simple and common substance that it is, has an enormous effect on everything. Part of the reason is its sheer abundance on this planet and its vital interaction with life itself. Moreover, its unique physical properties contribute to its extraordinary influence on the weather.

• Water is the only substance in the world that exists in all three phases—solid, liquid, and gas—at temperatures normally found at the earth's surface.

• Liquid water covers about two-thirds of the earth's surface. Its internal currents, vast heat reserve, interactions with the atmosphere, and varying rates of reflecting radiation have a great effect on worldwide weather.

• Bodies of water can absorb a tremendous amount of heat without becoming much warmer themselves—a property with far-reaching consequences for the weather.

• Condensation of water vapor to liquid is crucial to creating precipitation. In condensing, the water releases a great amount of energy (heat) into the atmosphere.

• Water's solid state, ice, is less dense than its liquid state. The result is that bodies of water freeze from the top down, instead of from the bottom up. Because ice reflects (rather than absorbs) such a high percentage of solar radiation, it fosters further cold conditions once they are established.

• The various crystalline forms of water contribute to a wide variety of precipitation types. When light is refracted through them, they display a dazzling array of halos, arcs, and other optical phenomena.

HYDROLOGIC CYCLE

Water circulates in varying forms throughout the world via innumerable routes and methods. Most of this water exists in liquid form in the oceans depository, but significant amounts are held captive in extensive ice sheets and glaciers, where they can remain withdrawn from active circulation for thousands of years. A small but vital percentage is found in the atmosphere.

The oceans contain some 331 million cubic miles of water, 96.5 percent of the world's supply. Freshwater reserves (including glaciers) hold 8.4 million cubic miles of water, 2.53 percent of the total supply. The volume of water in the atmosphere is a relatively tiny 3,096 cubic miles, only .001 percent of the total supply.

The earth's enormous water circulation system, called the *hydrologic cycle,* is powered by the processes of *evaporation, transpiration, sublimation, condensation,* and *precipitation.* All involve the changing and distribution of water as it is transported about the globe.

Hydrologic Cycle. *The hydrologic cycle describes the activity of water in the world: its phase changes, its vertical and horizontal movement, and its transfers between land, ocean, and sky.*

E	evaporation	I	infiltration	R	runoff
C	condensation	T	transpiration	GF	groundwater flow
S	sublimation	P	precipitation		

> FACT: Paradise, at Mt. Rainier, Washington, received 1224.5 inches of snow in the year from February 19, 1971, to February 8, 1972.

Evaporation. Evaporation—the conversion of liquid to vapor—is the largest source of atmospheric moisture. Evaporation largely functions near the earth's surface where rivers, lakes, and oceans offer saturated sources to the air.

Evaporation occurs whenever relatively dry air comes into contact with a relatively wet surface. Water molecules constantly transfer back and forth between liquid and vapor phases. If more molecules leave a lake than enter it, there is net evaporation. (If more enter than leave, there is net condensation.)

> FACT: Water first softens a seed's outer coat, then is absorbed into its inner tissue, triggering chemical reactions and swelling, which in turn, causes the seed to sprout.

A very important component of evaporation is its relationship to heat energy. The evaporation of water requires substantial heat that must be converted from the *sensible heat* of the surroundings (heat you can feel) into *latent heat* (heat you cannot feel) that is stored within the vapor itself, and the ambient temperature falls. Think of the chill on your skin after you get out of the pool, as water absorbs heat from your body to evaporate. When the vapor condenses back to a liquid, its latent heat is released as sensible heat into the environment. In other words, evaporation usually cools the local temperature, while condensation tends to raise it.

Transpiration. Transpiration, like evaporation, transfers moisture into the air, and refers to the contribution made by green growing plants. Groundwater absorbed from the soil is transported from the roots upward into the leaves. A chemical reation involving solar radiation and the chorophyll in the leaves releases water, and water vapor diffuses out of the plant and into the atmosphere.

Sublimation. Water vapor sometimes changes directly into ice, without passing through the intermediate liquid state. This is called *deposition,* and is the process by which frost forms on winter windowpanes. The reverse process, from ice to vapor, is called *sublimation,* a term that was formerly used to refer to both directions of the process. Sublimation is responsible for the way a snowbank may substantially diminish in strong sunshine without any noticeable melting.

Condensation. *Condensation* occurs when water in the atmosphere changes from vapor to liquid or from liquid to ice. In doing so, it forms clouds, fog, dew, and frost, and can lead to precipitation. Condensation is also an important component of the energy balance, releasing the latent heat of water.

The condensing process cannot start until the air first becomes supersaturated with a relative humidity slightly exceeding 100 percent. When this happens, the vapor begins to condense into extremely small water droplets that grow by collisions and by coalescing with others of their kind. In reality, however, the atmosphere is not a sterile place, and tiny particles of dust provide a surface on which water vapor can condense. The particles include sea salt, smoke, and the stuff of forest fires, volcanoes, and industrial pollution. These *condensation nuclei* facilitate cloud formation because their mere presence allows the formation of larger water droplets at lower supersaturation points.

These newly condensed droplets are so small that they are invisible and are held aloft by rising air. In still air, these microscopic drops slowly fall under the influence of gravity and rapidly evaporate when they enter air with less than 100 percent relative humidity. To become visible and constitute a cloud, they must grow to a size of 1 to 10 microns—still very tiny. To reach raindrop size, they must grow to a radius of about 1,000 microns, or 1 millimeter.

SCALES OF ATMOSPHERIC PHENOMENA

Size		Object
1 decameter	10^{-1} m	Largest hailstone
1 centimeter	10^{-2} m	Snowflake
1 millimeter	10^{-3} m	Small raindrop
100 microns	10^{-4} m	Ice cystal
10 microns	10^{-5} m	Large salt particle
1 micron	10^{-6} m	Cloud droplet
.01 micron	10^{-8} m	Smoke particle
1 nanometer	10^{-9} m	Small condensation nucleus
1 angstrom	10^{-10} m	Hydrogen atom

*Micron has been replaced by a new term, micro-meter, in international practice; however, it remains universally accepted and used in the atmospheric sciences.

In air colder than 32°F (0°C), water droplets freeze around particles in the atmosphere and form ice crystals. Under certain atmospheric conditions, ice can form by proceeding directly from vapor to solid, without ever becoming liquid. Ice crystals grow by bumping into supercooled water droplets or into other ice particles.

Precipitation. As water droplets or ice crystals grow in size, their falling velocity increases, and so does the tendency for growth through coalescing with other droplets or crystals. A typical raindrop is the end result of the coalition of upwards of one million cloud droplets. All water particles that eventually reach the ground are collectively called precipitation.

Three different processes produce precipitation. They depend on cloud temperature and on whether the water is liquid or frozen.

In an all-liquid process, collision and coalesence produce raindrops from tiny cloud droplets. The falling speed of the larger droplets exceeds those that are smaller, and as they fall and collide, smaller droplets merge with larger ones. This decreases the number of droplets while increasing their sizes and fall velocities, so they eventually grow to raindrop size and fall—to earth as precipitation.

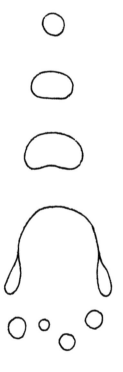

Raindrop Portrait. Real raindrops aren't the teardrops they are often depicted as. The drop's surface tension controls its shape as it falls; the smallest drops are held spherical (round). As the diameter increase, the drop's velocity exerts pressure on its bottom, causing it to distort into something shaped like a hamburger bun. As the drop's size increases past 9 mm, the shape grows into something like a parachute with a tube of water around its bottom edge, and then breaks up into smaller droplets, shown here in cross section.

METEOR – OLOGY

The modern science of meteorology is the study of the weather and atmospheric phenomena. To the ancient Greeks, however, the study of all heavenly phenomena was called *meteorologia,* and any projectile falling toward the earth from the sky was a *meteoron,* or "thing in the air." Quite descriptive, those old Greeks. To the Greeks, these "things" included raindrops, hailstones, and snowflakes as well as meteors and meteorites.

Where both liquid water and ice are present in the cloud, a different mechanism leads to precipitation. When a water droplet is near an ice crystal, differences in vapor pressure result in the droplet attaching to the ice crystal. The ice crystals develop at the expense of the water droplets, growing to a much larger size than the droplets. The ice crystals continue to collide with both droplets and other crystals, forming aggregates and snowflakes.

The all-ice process produces ice crystals at very low temperatures (under −22°F). The crystals grow slower than in the cloud that has both liquid water and ice. The usual result is only light precipitation of single ice crystals.

TYPICAL RAINDROP SIZES, DENSITIES, AND INTENSITIES

	Drop Diameter (in millimeters)	Density (in drops per square foot per second)	Intensity (in inches of precipitation per hour)
Fog	0.01	6,264,000	0.005
Mist	0.10	2,510	0.02
Drizzle	0.96	14	0.01
Light rain	1.24	26	0.04
Moderate rain	1.60	46	0.15
Heavy rain	2.05	46	0.60
Excessive rain	2.40	76	1.60
Cloudburst	2.85	113	4.00

HYDROMETEORS

Precipitation takes many forms, depending on temperature, humidity, and pressure. A general term, hydrometeors, is used to describe all types of condensation products including those such as dew and frost that technically are not precipitation.

Of course, the worldwide bearers of the profuse potpourri of precipitation, and hydrometeors themselves, are clouds. No understanding of the hydrologic cycle would be complete without a knowledge of cloud dynamics. For this, see chapter 4.

The following table defines the forms of hydrometeors and displays their symbols.

Suspended Hydrometeors

Fog	Suspended tiny cloud droplets (from a few microns to tens of microns in diameter), reducing visibility at the surface to less than 1 kilometer (roughly half a mile); appears as a whitish veil over the landscape. The relative humidity is usually near 100 percent.
≡	Sky discernible
≡	In patches
= =	Shallow fog (2 meters high or less)
= =	Shallow fog in patches
⍦	Fog depositing rime, sky discernible
⍦	Fog depositing rime, sky not discernible
Ice fog ↔	Suspended minute ice crystals, reducing visibility at the surface; crystals often glitter in the sunshine and produce luminous pillars and small halos.

Suspended Hydrometeors *(continued)*

Mist	Suspended microscopic water droplets, reducing visibility less than fog in a thin, grayish veil; relative humidity is often less than 95 percent.

Falling Hydrometeors

Drizzle	Water droplets less than .5 mm diameter that fall with accumulation rates of less than 1 mm per hour.
Rain	Water droplets greater than .5 mm diameter that fall with accumulation rates greater than 1 mm per hour.
Virga	Water drops or ice particles that evaporate before reaching the ground. This can be seen as dark vertical streaks under a cloud that often fade to near-horizontal before disappearing into thin air.
Ice prisms	Very small, unbranched ice crystals; mainly visible when they glitter in the sunshine, and known as *diamond dust*. Occur most frequently in polar regions in very cold, stable conditions.
Snow grains	Very small, opaque white ice particles, less than 1 mm in diameter; usually fairly flat or elongated; they fall in very small quantities from stratus or fog and do not bounce or shatter.
Snow pellets	Opaque white, spherical or conical snow grains that grow by aggregation with other ice particles, showing no crystalline structure; 2 to 5 mm in diameter. Also known as *graupel* or *soft hail,* the brittle pellets bounce and break upon striking the ground.

Falling Hydrometeors *(continued)*

Ice pellets	1. Small translucent ice particles 5 mm or less in diameter, formed either by rain freezing during its descent to the ground or by snow that melts and refreezes before reaching the surface; also called *sleet*.
	2. Snow pellets encased in a thin layer of ice formed by accretion of freezing droplets or by the melting and refreezing of the pellet; less than 5 mm diameter; formerly called *small hail*.
Hail	Hard, round, or irregularly shaped ice conglomerations with concentric layers of clear and white ice formed by alternate layers of rime and glaze; greater than 5 mm diameter.
Snow	White or translucent crystalline structures usually resembling flakes. Snow forms under many different conditions and undergoes continuous changes as it falls. Snow can be further classified according to crystalline shape, structure, and liquid moisture content (wet or dry snow).

Deposited

Fog droplets	Fog or cloud droplets deposited directly on the ground or on an object.
Dew	Water that has condensed directly on the ground or on an object.

Deposited *(continued)*

Frost	Ice that has sublimated directly on the ground or an object, usually in the form of scales, needles, features, or fans; also called *hoarfrost* or *white frost*.
White dew	Dew that has frozen after its formation; more opaque than frost.
Glaze	A clear, smooth coating of ice formed by rain or drizzle that freezes relatively slowly upon impact with the ground or on an exposed object; also called *silver thaw*.
Rime	Ice formed by rapid freezing of supercooled water droplets coming into contact with an exposed object; three types: 1. soft rime: fragile rime consisting mainly of thin needles or scales of ice. 2. hard rime: granular rime, usually white, with crystalline branches of ice grains separated by entrapped air. 3. clear ice: smooth compact rime, usually transparent with ragged surface, resembling glaze.

Raised by the Wind

Drifting snow	Snow particles raised by the wind to heights of less than 2 meters above the ground; low objects are veiled or hidden by moving snow. Moderate or heavy drifting snow

Raised by the Wind *(continued)*

Blowing snow	Snow particles raised by the wind to heights greater than 2 meters above the ground; sometimes sufficient to veil the sky and even the sun. Horizontal visibility is generally very poor, and vertical visibility is diminished. Moderate or heavy blowing snow Drifting and blowing snow
Spray	Water droplets torn by the wind from the surface of a large body of water, generally from the crests of waves, and carried a short distance into the air. When the water surface is rough, the spray may be accompanied by foam.

FACT: Black frost is the internal freezing of plant materials without the formation of external ice crystals, and refers to the frozen vegetation's blackened appearance.

BASIC SNOW CLASSIFICATION

While it may very well be true that no two snowflakes are exactly alike, snow can be classified according to its basic crystalline structure. Flakes that arrive at the ground are usually clusters of many individual ice crystals. The type of crystal is determined mainly by the temperature in which it forms and secondarily by the saturation vapor pressure (see page 65) with respect to ice.

The following table describes basic crystalline shapes of snow. Composite crystals form as growing crystals move into regions of differing temperature and supersaturation conditions. As long as a crystal or snowflake exists, it changes by growth, riming, aggregation, melting, and—after falling to the ground—continuing metamorphosis as it ages.

THE SHAPES OF SNOW

Shape Name	Description	Temp. Range °C	°F
Plates	Thin, solid or semisolid hexagons, lengths shorter than diameters; rarely clumped.	0 to −4	32 to 24.8
Columns	Flat-ended, transparent or translucent, lengths longer than diameters; solid at lesser saturations, hollow at greater saturations.	−3 to −8; less than −22	26.6 to 17.6; less than −7.6
Capped columns	Columns with both ends terminated by hexagonal plates; plates sometimes positioned midway as well.	−3 to −25	26.6 to −13
Needles	Long slender shafts with hexagonal cross section often with sharp irregular points, usually clumped.	−4 to −6	24.8 to 21.2
Sector plates	Hexagonal plates with branched arms; thin or thick; skeletal with cusped borders, or flat and solid.	−10 to −12; −16 to −22	14 to 10.4; 3.2 to −7.6

THE SHAPES OF SNOW *(continued)*

Shape Name	Description	Temp. Range °C	°F
Dendrites	*Plane:* flat star-shaped single crystals or clumps. *Spatial:* complex crystals with fernlike arms radiating from the center.	–12 to –16	10.4 to 3.2
Irregular	Small balls or lumps of ice, separate or as agglomerations.	varying	

MOISTURE MEASUREMENTS

People love to talk about the weather, and moisture statistics are a favorite topic. How much rain or snow fell? And what's the relative humidity?

Rain. How much rain is an inch of rain? A good question. Suppose you put a can in your backyard during a storm and you catch an inch of rain. How much would you have? A pint maybe? It all depends on the shape and size of your can, you reckon. But you've seen all the shapes and sizes of rain gauges; surely one inch in a large gauge is more rain than one inch in a small one. What gives?

Fortunately there is a standard, and it has nothing to do with the gauge itself. One inch of rain is defined as the amount of rain that would cover one acre of impervious material to a depth of one inch. Now we can talk about actual quantity: One inch of rain covering an acre amounts to about 27,000 gallons.

But when the forecaster predicts or reports one inch of rain, is he or she talking about 27,000 gallons of water? Not likely. Because a forecast area includes hundreds of thousands of acres, and because rainfall varies depending on local topography, temperature, wind direction, and other factors, the forecaster is talking about the average depth of the precipitation over the forecast area. At any point above the surface there may be one inch of water.

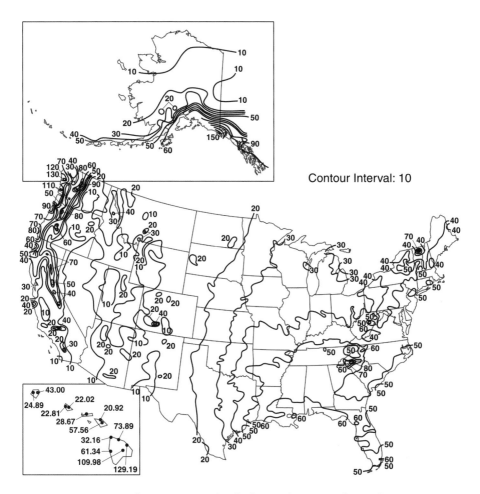

Contour Interval: 10

U.S. Mean Annual Precipitation (Inches). Based on Normal Period, 1961–1990

Rain gauges do vary in size and shape, and therefore in the actual amount of water they collect. But the amount doesn't matter. What's important is having a standard of measurement. As long as your can has straight vertical sides, the collection area-to-volume ratio is 1:1 and an inch of rain in your can is an inch of rain, period. (And don't be confused by the gauges with slanted sides or funnels. They are simply constructed with a correct ratio that makes small amounts easier to measure.)

FACT: The highest average annual rainfall occurs in Mawsynram, Meghalaya, India: 467.5 inches.

Snow. Snowfall is measured and reported by its accumulation on the ground, but its melted amount is recorded as its water equivalent in the precipitation total. The moisture content of most continental U.S. cyclones average between 6–10 inches of snow depth to one inch of liquid precipitation.

THE WATER IN SNOW

Snow Classification	Liquid Content	Description	Approx. Snow Depth Equiv. to 1" Precip.
Dry	0%	Individual snow grains have little tendency to adhere even when pressed together.	100"–33"
Moist	Less than 3%	Water is not visible even under 10X magnification; exhibits distinct tendency to stick together when lightly crushed.	More than 33"
Wet	3-8%	Water can be seen between adjacent snow grains under 10X magnification, but cannot be pressed out by moderate hand squeezing.	33"–7"
Very wet	8-15%	Water can be pressed out by moderate hand squeezing, but there is still appreciable air confined in the pores.	7"–2.5"
Slush	More than 15%	The snow is flooded with water and contains a relatively small amount of air.	Less than 2.5"

Humidity. Water in the atmosphere—the humidity—is the most difficult of weather components to measure. Humidity measurements are of two types: those that measure the actual quantity of water in the air, and those that compare the actual amount of vapor to the potential amount that could exist if the air were saturated. The most useful measure in amateur weather forecasting is the second type, the comparative ratio of the *relative humidity.*

FACT: The expandable skin of the saguaro cactus can double its girth during the rainy season, enabling the cactus to soak up as much as 200 gallons of water during a single storm.

Relative humidity actually compares two pressures: the *vapor pressure* (the pressure of the air attributed to its water vapor content) and the *saturation vapor pressure* (the pressure of water vapor in saturated air). The ratio of vapor pressure to saturation vapor pressure is expressed as a percentage.

A small parcel of air in contact with a water surface can be defined as saturated when the number of water molecules evaporating into the air equal the number of vapor molecules condensing out of the air: Water and air have reached an equilibrium. But if the air warms, the liquid water molecules at the surface absorb heat, gain energy, and move faster. Because of the additional heat, the air and the water are no longer in equilibrium. More water molecules are now able to evaporate into the air, and a greater number of vapor molecules are required to reach a new equilibrium between water and air. Similarly, as the air cools, so do the vapor molecules. Their average speed slows, and more return to liquid water than leave it, until a lower equilibrium is reached.

This observation is commonly expressed as the "holding" capacity of the air: Warm air can "hold" more moisture than can cold air. However, while it may an easy way to describe it, air has zero holding capacity for water, warm or cold. Remember that the moisture content of air is not dependent on the air temperature, but on the presence and pressure exerted by the molecules of water vapor. We can perhaps better think of air as "containing" water vapor much in the same way that it "contains" dust particles, or molecules of oxygen or nitrogen.

Relative humidity is measured with a *psychrometer,* consisting of a pair of thermometers. One is called the *dry bulb,* and measures the air temperature. The other is the *wet bulb,* and has a wet wick of cotton on its bulb. As water evaporates from the wick, it absorbs heat from the air immediately surrounding the wet bulb. The drier the air, the greater the evaporation, the lower the temperature reading of the wet bulb, and the lower the relative humidity. Should the air be near saturation (100 percent relative humidity), very little evaporation occurs, and the wet bulb temperature is nearly equal to that of the dry bulb. A table is consulted to obtain the relative humidity from the wet and dry bulb readings.

Another useful humidity measurement is the *dew point,* the temperature at which air becomes saturated and condensation (or dew) forms. This occurs when the saturation vapor pressure over water equals the actual vapor pressure of the air. The dew point is a convenient measure for meteorologists to report and compare the humidity of the air at various points on the surface, as well as at higher altitudes.

Because the capacity of the air to contain water in the vapor phase is proportional to the temperature and the pressure, many aspects of the weather are affected by this relationship. For example, as a rising parcel of air expands and cools, its lower temperature and pressure may produce saturation conditions, and a cloud forms. As air cools overnight, dew may form with no substantial change in the pressure. Similarly, a stable layer of air at the surface may develop fog simply because the temperature drops, without any change in pressure. Correspondingly, a rise in the local temperature may quickly dissipate the fog. Together, the *ménage à trois* of heat, pressure, and moisture is responsible for the ever-evolving, constantly capricious, wonderful ways of weather.

OBSERVATIONS AND ACTIVITIES

Transpiration Trap. The intricate processes of transpiration and saturation are invisible. But here's a way for you to see them.

Materials: Wide-mouth jar or drinking glass, a mowed lawn.

To Know: Transpiration is the loss of water vapor from vegetation, normally dispersed directly into the atmosphere. Saturation of air results when the air can absorb no more water vapor.

To Do: Place the jar or glass upside down on green grass; wait a few minutes and observe the inside of the glass. Moisture transpiring from the growing grass (and water evaporating from the soil) is continually added to the air under the glass. Soon the tiny atmosphere becomes saturated and cannot contain any more vapor. The excess condenses on the sides of the glass.

Try the procedure again on varying surfaces, such as soil, dry grass, or a potted flower, to observe the results. Try again under varying weather conditions: bright sunlight, overcast sky, cold and warm conditions. Record the elapsed time until droplets are observed. How does this rate of transpiration and/or evaporation vary with the weather conditions? with types of vegetation or ground cover?

Making Dew. You can force dew out of the air, and calculate the dew point.

Materials: Metal can or tray, ice cubes, water, thermometer, pencil, paper.

To Know: The dew point is the temperature at which the air becomes saturated (100 percent relative humidity) and excess moisture begins to condense, forming dew on exposed objects. If the dew point is at or below the freezing point of water, frost forms instead.

To Do: Record the air temperature. Nearly fill the can with water, making sure the outside of the can is dry. Insert the thermometer into the water, and add ice, a little at a time, gently stirring with the thermometer. Because of the metal can's ability to readily conduct heat (or the lack of it), the air immediately surrounding the can cools to the same temperature as the water. Observe the outside of the can; as soon as droplets form, record the temperature of the water, which is also the air's dew point.

While you cannot measure the dew point in the sky by this method, you can note the height at which it occurs by observing the flat bottoms of growing cumulus clouds. The rising, cooling air reaches its dew point at that altitude, the vapor begins to condense into droplets, and the cloud grows upward from that point. What can you deduce about how cloud base heights correspond to the relative humidity of the air and/or the temperature profiles above you?

Catch a Falling Snowflake. With the right background and a little magnification, you can get a good look at a snowflake.

Materials: Embroidery hoop and black velvet (a piece of black construction paper on cardboard will also work), toothpick, magnifying lens, 6-inch ruler.

To Know: Snowflakes are usually aggregates of many smaller crystals, which develop under particular temperature and humidity conditions in the cloud they fell from.

To Do: Insert the black cloth in the embroidery hoop and catch falling snowflakes on its surface. Move them about with a toothpick and examine them under the magnifying lens. What is the average size of the snowflakes? How many different crystal forms can you identify? What information can you infer about the cloud conditions that produced them? Take several observations during a storm's passage: How do the crystalline shapes change as the storm progresses?

Tell Me, Diary, Dew. Keep a dew and frost diary, making notations of other weather conditions whenever dew or frost forms overnight, as well as the weather that follows that day. What correlations can you make between cloud cover and dew or frost formation? From your records, determine if the following weather proverb is true. Why or why not?

> When dew is on the grass
> Rain will never come to pass.
> When grass is dry at morning light
> Look for rain before the night.

Get up early to examine the crystalline frost pattern on a windowpane with a magnifying lens. Melt a funny face in it with your fingertips. Explain that you are demonstrating heat conduction.

CHAPTER 4

Clouds:
From Both Sides
Now

The most visible manifestation of the weather is the endlessly mutating variety of clouds. Riding the winds and delivering the juice of the sky, clouds also portend the future. In their formation and development, their shapes and patterns, and their travel and distribution, we can find a more thorough understanding of the nature of the weather and its far-reaching influences.

Clouds come in an infinite variety of shapes, but a limited number of forms. Recognizing this, a basic cloud classification system was developed by the English pharmacist Luke Howard in 1803 even before the atmospheric processes involved were clearly understood. Using Latin names to describe what he saw, his work remains the basis of today's system, with minor improvements: *cumulus* (a heap, pile, or mound) for convective clouds; *stratus* (spread or strewn) for layered clouds; *cirrus* (filament) for fibrous clouds; and *nimbus* (rain cloud) for storm clouds.

Today we recognize two basic atmospheric processes that develop three basic types of clouds: local convection (upward heat flow) producing scattered individual heaped *cumuliform clouds;* large-scale lifting producing the widespread sheet formation known as *stratiform clouds;* and a combination of these forces producing clouds showing elements of both mechanisms, the *duo-process clouds.* Clouds are also categorized according to the range of heights at which they frequently form.

Clouds range from sea level and the earth's surface up to the tropopause— as high as 60,000 feet (about 11 miles) in the tropics. Altostratus and nimbostratus often extend upward into the high level; nimbostratus often lowers to the surface as well. Cumulus and cumulonimbus have their bases in the lowest group, but their vertical extent may push their tops into the middle and high levels. The table on the following page gives the ranges of approximate elevations at which each type of cloud occurs most frequently in the polar, temperate, and tropical regions of the atmosphere.

CUMULIFORM CLOUDS: POPCORN HEAPS

The *cumuliform* family of heap clouds are convective in nature, as warmed air rises and expands and condensation forms cauliflower-shaped domes with flat bottoms. The flattened bottoms mark the level where rising air reaches saturation and condensation begins. The degree of instability and lifting and moisture content determine how high the cloud may continue to grow above that level.

The smallest cumulus clouds pop up with dimensions of just a few yards wide and high. These little white clouds show settled weather and usually appear in late mornings and early afternoons, after the day's sunshine warms

HOW CLOUDS STACK UP

	Polar Regions Altitude range, in:			Temperate Regions Altitude range, in:			Tropical Regions Altitude range in:		
	km	miles	feet	km	miles	feet	km	miles	feet
High clouds: cirrus cirrostratus cirrocumulus	3–8	2–5	10,000–26,000	5–13	3–8	16,000–45,000	6–18	4–11	21,000–60,000
Middle clouds: altocumulus altostratus nimbostratus	2–4	1.25–2.5	6,500–13,000	2–7	1.25–4.25	6,500–23,000	2–8	1.25–5	6,500–26,000
Low clouds: fogs stratus stratocumulus cumulus cumulonimbus	0–2	0–1.25	surface to 6,500	0–2	0–1.25	surface to 6,500	0–2	0–1.25	surface to 6,500

the surface air a bit. The warmed air becomes an invisible rising bubble, called a *thermal,* seeking a level of temperature equilibrium as it rises and cools and its relative humidity increases. If the thermal reaches saturation, condensation occurs and the cumulus forms. The latent heat of condensation is released inside the thermal, raising its temperature and increasing its buoyancy. Eventually the thermal cools to the point where its temperature is no longer warmer than that of the surrounding air, and it stops rising. The stability in the atmosphere generally limits growth of these *fair-weather cumulus* (also known as *cumulus humilis*) to about 3,000 feet. These clouds never produce precipitation.

At the boundaries of the fair-weather cumulus, there is always mixing between moist and dry air, with simultaneous condensation and evaporation. Sharply defined edges of the cloud show expansion and growth, where condensation is strong. But when the rate of evaporation into the drier air exceeds the rate of condensation, the air cools and sinks, and the cloud edges fray and tear.

The evaporation and sinking motion on the outside of the cloud keep its width nearly constant and prohibit any other clouds from forming near its own boundaries, which is why small cumulus are always separated by clear air.

When all the air inside the thermal becomes mixed or diluted with dry air, the cloud begins to sink and deteriorate into *fractocumulus* (from the Latin *fractus,* meaning "broken"). The constant mixing and evaporation limit life spans to mere minutes, but the continual resurgence of new thermals and new cumulus humilis give the effect of little change over time.

Middle-level cumulus show more energy and instability in the atmosphere, as the same process that developed the fair-weather cumulus is allowed to continue vertical growth. Individual *towering cumulus* (also known as *cumulus mediocris*) clouds show many rising cells that are in turn composed of still smaller cells, all at different stages of development in which the overall condensation outstrips the overall evaporation. The general air motion is upward within the cloud, with localized sinking motions, and the cauliflower appearance takes on a distinct domed tower shape. The base remains generally flat, but cloud tops may reach as high as 19,000 feet.

In unstable air, the towering cumulus may sprout very quickly and generate much greater height than width. These turret-like formations have inspired their name of *cumulus castellanus.* If the turrets evaporate rather quickly, appearing like flocks or tufts of wool, they are descriptively called *cumulus floccus.*

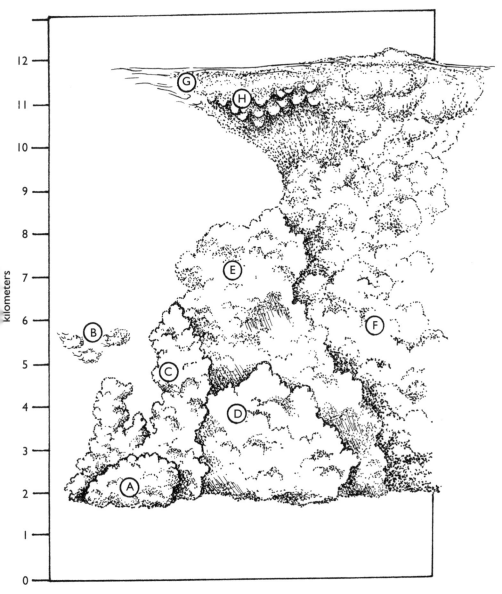

Cumuliform Clouds. *The vertical scale shows approximate and typical heights.*

a. cumulus humilis (fair-weather cumulus)
b. cumulus floccus
c. cumulus castellanus
d. cumulus mediocris (towering cumulus)

e. cumulus congestus
f. cumulonimbus
g. anvil
h. mamma

FACT: The plant known as the African everlasting opens its flowers when the relative humidity is 5 percent or less, partially closes them at 65 percent, and shuts them completely at 76 percent.

In a more unstable environment, a towering cumulus will swell with hundreds of thousands of individual convective cells, as a huge amount of energy is released into the air through latent heat of condensation, making the rising air more buoyant. This cycle feeds on itself, building bulging *cumulus congestus* clouds as high as 45,000 feet.

At such high altitudes, water droplets develop into ice crystals, marking the defining transition to *cumulonimbus* clouds. High winds at this upper level where convection is capped may draw out a flattened, wispy *anvil* top to the cloud. The anvil is a separate ice cloud produced by the lifting of a layer of air above the cumulonimbus, and is actually a type of cirrus cloud. The cumulonimbus is often very dark and may have low ragged clouds sweeping along; a large base may stretch a few dozen miles wide. Heavy precipitation is usual. An especially intense cumulonimbus may develop downward protuberances on its anvil called *mamma*, indicating very strong downdrafts that mix moist, cloudy air with drier surrounding air.

STRATIFORM CLOUDS

Layered clouds have no convective warming and rising involved in their formation, are much shorter than they are wide, and last much longer than cumulus clouds. Appearing as featureless sheets of clouds, they may extend in width from 5 to 500 miles or more, yet their thickness may be no more than 1,500 to 3,000 feet. One altostratus cloud may spread over more than 350,000 square miles—about the size of Texas, Oklahoma, and Kansas combined.

Layered, or stratiform, clouds are formed by forced lifting of stable air on a large scale; they can form at any altitude. Air that gradually ascends over a denser layer of air, or over a gentle incline of land, will expand and cool, allowing condensation to permeate the entire layer. Air convergence and its associated uplift does the same. Other processes produce the various types of fogs, which are simply stratus clouds on the ground.

CLOUDINESS FORECASTS: THE TRANSLATION

Nebulous Term	Sky Coverage
Clear = Sunny	10% or less
Mostly clear = Mostly sunny	10%–20%
Partly sunny = Partly cloudy	30%–60%
Fair	40% or less
Mostly cloudy	70%–80%
Cloudy	90%–100%

Most stratiform clouds form in the ascent of air associated with cyclones in the boundary zone between cold and warm air masses. As the large horizontal mass of warm air is lifted over the cold and denser air, the layer expands, cools, and condenses. The earliest signal of an approaching warm front are the very highest clouds. Found at heights over 40,000 feet near the top of the troposphere are the wispy *cirrus* clouds, composed entirely of very small, sparse ice crystals, which accounts for their transparency. Unlike most stratiform clouds, layers of cirrus clouds are not continuous. White and delicate in appearance, they average about 5,000 feet thick.

In addition to the wispy, filament form, *cirrus* clouds may take on a tufted or bent whisk-broom shape, when ice crystals grow large enough to fall out of the cloud as dark, vertical streaks. These streaks are usually curved or slanted, shaped by changes in the horizontal wind. Popularly known as *mare's tails,* this form has also been tagged with Latin: *cirrus uncinus.*

CONTRAILS

Water clouds that are formed by air motion following an aircraft, or the condensation of water in the exhaust, are called condensation trails—contrails. Those that quickly freeze at −40°F or lower are the ones that linger in the air long after the jet has passed. With time, most of the trail evaporates into the surrounding air. But where the air is saturated for ice and not for water, these contrails may be stretched by the wind into extensive sheets of new cirrus clouds.

The cirrus of the warm front are followed by a very thin, transparent layer of *cirrostratus* some 5 miles high. Also made of ice crystals, the cirrostratus is so thin at times that it may be invisible, yet sunlight shining through it may reveal its presence by the appearance of halos as it refracts through the six-sided crystals. It is never thick enough to prevent objects on the ground from casting a shadow, certainly when the sun is at least 30 degrees above the horizon.

Cirrostratus is followed by lower and thicker *altostratus,* 3 to 4 miles (16,000 to 21,000 feet) high and about 1 to 2 miles thick. Altostratus is generally not a precipitation producer, although it may happen when ice crystals at the top of the cloud fall through supercooled droplets in the lower portion of the cloud to create snow or drizzle. These clouds appear gray or bluish, fibrous, striated, or lightly striped. *Coronas,*—brightly colored rings about the sun or moon—may be created by light diffracted through the small water droplets of the altostratus.

An altostratus cloud thickens and darkens as its base lowers close to the ground with the approach of a weather-front boundary. As it becomes thick enough to mask the sun and begins to produce rain or snow, it becomes the true rain cloud, the primary precipitation producer of the atmosphere: *nimbostratus.*

With a base at about 6,500 feet, nimbostratus can extend several miles vertically, often consisting of supercooled droplets and ice particles at the cold top and water droplets in the lower, warmer bottom. This is an ideal setup for precipitation through the growth of ice crystals. With the air supersaturated with respect to ice, droplets evaporate and ice crystals eventually grow large enough to fall as snow.

Whether the crystals reach the ground as snow depends on the temperature of the air through which they fall. If the melting level occurs inside the cloud, it is visible as a change in the cloud's color: The area above the melting line is a darker color than that below it. Most nimbostratus precipitation that reaches the ground as rain originated as snow. Rain-moistened air beneath the nimbostratus often develops small, ragged and dark clouds known as *scud.* At times these may merge into a continuous layer extending up to the base of the nimbostratus.

Stratus is the term reserved for the lowest stratiform clouds, those widespread and uniformly gray layers below 5,000 feet. Stratus clouds are often the result of fog lifting off the surface, although they also commonly develop under the precipitating influences of altostratus, nimbostratus, or cumulo-

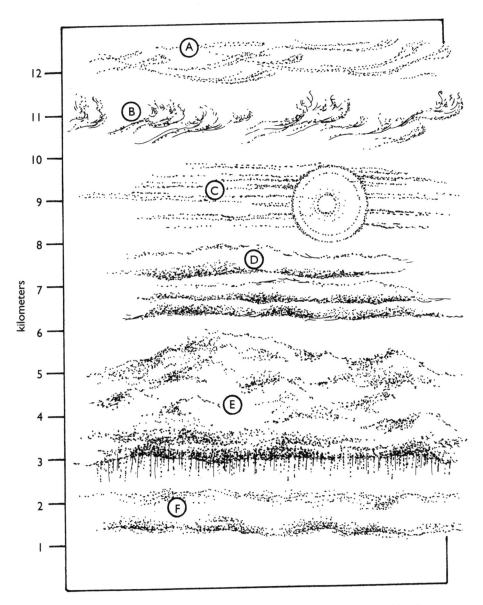

Stratiform Clouds. *The vertical scale shows approximate and typical heights.*

a. cirrus

b. cirrus uncinus (mare's tails)

c. cirrostratus

d. altostratus

e. nimbostratus

f. stratus

READING THE CLOUDS

The height of the lowest cloud in the sky is called the ceiling and is measured by a device called the *rotating beam ceilometer.* From it, an intense beam of light is projected up to the cloud base, where the beam is reflected back to earth. A photoelectric cell detector located at a known distance from the projector scans continuously to detect the illuminated spot, then transmits a signal to an indicator. The device, used both day and night, provides critical information to aviators.

The direction of cloud movement, and therefore wind direction at cloud height, can be determined with an instrument called a *nephoscope* (from the Greek *nephos,* meaning "cloud"). A simple nephoscope uses a grid or a crosspiece comb of rods attached to the top of a post eight to ten feet high. The post is free to rotate, and the observer turns the rods to parallel the direction of cloud movement, then notes the compass direction. The direction of winds aloft may reveal the direction of movement of large-scale features of cyclones and squall lines.

nimbus. Consisting of small water droplets, and too warm to initiate ice crystals, the stratus cloud is unable to produce much rain or snow; drizzle is its more likely output. The stratus is usually capped by a temperature inversion that inhibits vertical growth. When the stratus breaks up, it forms a new category of cloud, which combines the processes of both layers and heaps.

DUO-PROCESS CLOUDS: LAYERED POPCORN COMBO

The third type of cloud formation combines aspects of both cumuliform and stratiform.

As a sheet of stratus, contained under a temperature inversion, begins to radiate heat to the air above it, the top of the cloud cools. Rising moist air creates a downward motion of cooler, drier air that sinks into the cloud and begins the breakup of the stratus into *stratocumulus.* Small convective cells, with their associated rising and sinking air parcels, produce characteristic thick and thin regions of a lumpy-looking cloud 5,000 to 10,000 feet up. When stratocumulus fill the sky, they often appear in long, heavy ridges, looking like sheets of corrugated roofing.

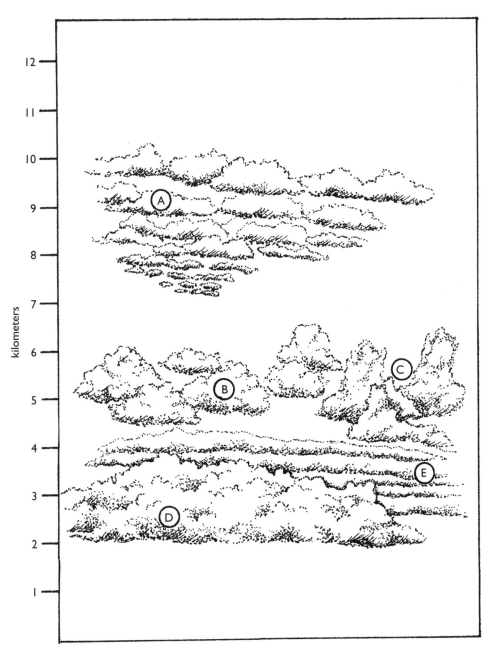

Duo-Process Clouds. *The vertical scale shows approximate and typical heights.*

a. cirrocumulus
b. altocumulus

c. altocumulus castellanus
d. stratocumulus

e. stratocumulus undulatis

Turbulence and Mountain-generated Clouds

lenticular wave clouds

rotor clouds

a. Wave clouds *appear in the crests of a stable air flow that undulates after having been forced over a mountaintop or rolling terrain. They are often polished into smooth lens-shaped billows that are then called* lenticularis. *A* rotor cloud *shaped like a long cylinder sometimes forms in a turbulent eddy on the lee side.*

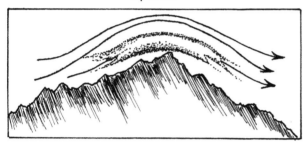

cap cloud

banner cloud

b. A cap cloud *may form in cool, dry air that has been lifted to its dew point over a mountain or by a rising thermal. The cloud appears to be stationary, although it continues to grow on the windward side and dissipate on the leeward side. The same result may occur when the strong growth of a towering cumulus obstructs moist upper-level winds. As the winds are forced over the rising thermal, the cap cloud formed is called* pileus, *and may feature several stacked together.*

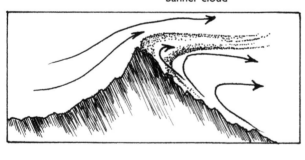

c. Turbulent lift created on the lee side may force moist air to condense in a banner cloud *appearing like a pennant waving from the crest.*

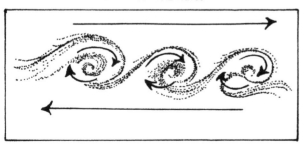

Kelvin-Helmholz waves

d. Strong wind shear in the upper levels may produce a special kind of cirrus that appear much like breaking ocean waves. Vertical eddies produce a distinctive undulating pattern known as Kelvin-Helmholtz waves. Without sufficient moisture to form the visible clouds, the eddies create dangerous clear air turbulence.

Being warm clouds, stratocumulus produce little precipitation. What does coalesce and fall as drizzle usually evaporates below the cloud and does not reach the ground. This action cools the air below the cloud, establishing stability there, cutting off any upward transport of air and moisture, and ensuring its dissipation.

Should a layer of stratocumulus divide into smaller units, *altocumulus* may develop. Frequently formed between 12,000 and 20,000 feet, altocumulus clouds appear as white or gray sheets or patches with shaded, rolled masses that look like puffy cotton balls, which may or may not be connected.

The altocumulus pattern appears in a higher, thinner form in the subfreezing temperatures over 20,000 feet as *cirrocumulus,* composed of super-cooled water and ice crystals. Small convection currents produce the characteristic ripples that reminded old-time mariners of fish scales. Their old proverb "Mackerel sky and mare's tails / Make lofty ships carry low sails" is perceptive in that cirrocumulus are associated with the approach of warm fronts and may precede thunderstorms.

Holding your fist at arm's length can help you identify the duo-process clouds. Stratocumulus lumps will be the size of your fist or larger. Altocumulus puffs will appear the size of your thumb. Cirrocumulus scales will match your thumbnail in apparent size.

FOG: MIST SOUP

The lowest clouds are grounded. Composed of tiny droplets like most other clouds, fog is simply a cloud that forms on or sinks to the surface of the earth. In temperatures less than −22°F, ice crystals may form an ice fog. The thick-

---

IN A FOG

Certain plants have adapted to obtaining needed moisture from fogs. Northern California's 300-foot-tall redwood trees pull moisture from the frequent fog directly into their needles. Spanish moss and other "air plants" absorb water from the air by use of special absorbent hairs along their stems and leaves. Taking inspiration from the plant kingdom, there have been recent attempts to extract useful moisture from fogs in rainless places such as the Atacama Desert of Peru and Chile by erecting huge screens along the coastline in the wind flow to intercept the tiny fog droplets.

Radiation Fog. *The most common fog over land is* radiation fog, *a cooling fog, which usually forms in still, moist air overnight as the earth radiates heat away and the air cools to its dew point. Radiation fog occurs most frequently in valley bottoms where cool air accumulates after draining down hillsides.*

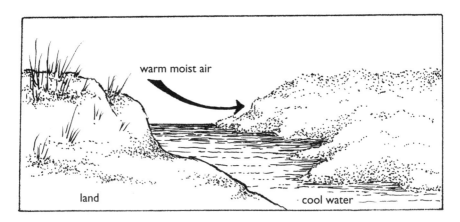

warm moist air

land

cool water

Advection Fog. *Advection fog another cooling fog, forms when moist air flows over a cold surface; most sea fogs are advection fogs. Advection-radiation fog, called* ground fog, *arises due to both influences and is generally only a few feet thick. At times, ground fog may sink into valleys and is then called* valley fog. *Aerial and satellite photos have often shown the soft and branching beauty of fog settled in the drainage pattern of a watershed.*

Upslope Fog. *A third type of cooling fog is formed as air is forced upward along a surface and expands and cools, and its vapor condenses to form an* upslope fog. *Mount Washington in New Hampshire, which forces both easterly and westerly winds to rise over its summit, experiences upslope fog more than 300 days each year.*

ness of fog depends on the size and density of the water droplets. Fog thickness is, of course, a prime consideration because it limits visibility and can result in traffic accidents, airport closures, and other serious problems.

Fogs are categorized according to the processes that produce them. They are further classified as cooling or warming fogs.

Fogs affect both the weather and the climate. On clear days, a fog will reflect sunlight and retard warming and the tendency for convection. Thunderstorms rarely grow over areas that had morning fog. Extensive fogs found off the west coasts of continents cool the climate by reflecting significant amounts of solar radiation.

Fog can be both intensified and dissipated through human intervention. The famous London "pea soup" fogs were exacerbated by widespread burning of coal and its resulting airborne particulates. Now that coal-burning has been greatly restricted, London gets 50 percent more sunshine during the winter months.

Fog dissipation can be attempted if the fog is shallow and the wind is gentle. This is sometimes feasible at airports, where helicopters hover over the fog layer, stirring the warmer air above with that at the surface to evaporate it. Another procedure is to seed the fog with salt particles or ice crystals to make the fog droplets grow large enough to fall out. To be successful, these expensive approaches must be done continually while conditions persist; otherwise, fog from the surrounding area quickly closes in as a reminder of nature's obvious advantage in size and might.

Steam Fog. *Warming fogs may form as air warms. Cold air passing over a warm water surface produces* steam fog, *also known as* sea smoke. *Water vapor rising from the comparatively warmer water rises into the cooler air and rapidly condenses into fog droplets.*

Frontal Fog. *Frontal fog is produced in the passage of a warm front as warm rain falls into colder air below, and the evaporating raindrops saturate the colder layer. This warming fog occurs more frequently after a prolonged period of precipitation from winter storms.*

OBSERVATIONS AND ACTIVITIES

Picture the Weather. The never-ending sky panorama is an excellent subject for the art of photography.

Materials: 35-mm camera with variable lens, film, filters, tripod, good eye, good luck.

To Know: Because weather is a "happenin' thing," a good photographer always has a camera handy. All the rules of good photography apply to create stunning sky scenes. The use of certain filters can enhance desired results. (See the sidebar on sky photography in this chapter.)

To Do: Get a feel for the capabilities of your camera, lens, and filter combinations. To start, take several shots of each cloud or sky subject: one at a regular setting, another a half-stop above, and a third at a half-stop below. Decide what exposure best suits your taste and objectives. For each photo, record the date, time, location, camera direction, aperture, and speed, plus film type and film speed and filter type, as well as field notes of current weather, cloud type, heights, and direction of motion.

Try these projects:

Cloud almanac. Capture specimens of each of the types of cumuliform, stratiform, and duo-process clouds described earlier in this chapter.

Sunrise, sunset. It's gotta be color; be wary of overexposure.

Snow crystals. Transfer collected specimens with a toothpick to chilled glass slides and shoot through a microscope lens. (See the *Peterson Field Guide to the Atmosphere,* by V. J. Schaefer and J. A. Day, Houghton Mifflin, 1981, page 297, for more information on microphotography.)

Lightning. Requires gambling with time exposures; work safely.

Storms and severe weather. As with photographing lightning, use common sense and stay safe.

Time-lapse. Record the birth and death of a small cumulus cloud, the advance of a warm front, the full play of twilight, and other weather dramas.

Follow the Clouds. You can determine the direction of cloud movement by building and using your own nephoscope.

Materials: Tools for cutting, measuring, and finishing wood; wood glue, wood screws, 1" x 8' dowel, ½" x 4' dowel, 2" x 4" lumber and other wood scraps, compass, post-hole digger.

To Know: Clouds often move in directions that are different from the wind at ground level.

SKY PHOTOGRAPHY

Most good cameras with variable lenses can take adequate pictures of the sky. The sharpest images are produced by tripod-mounted cameras, regardless of shutter speeds or lens lengths. Automatic cameras control settings of exposure, aperture, and focus, and are programmed to take good pictures in most circumstances—but they can be tricked by certain conditions to perform poorly. Manual single-lens reflex cameras offer the greatest versatility to the knowledgeable operator under the most diverse conditions.

While black-and-white films can produce dramatic skyscapes, color is essential to capture halos, rainbows, and other optical effects. A film's sensitivity to light (its speed) is indicated by its ISO number (formerly ASA). Slower films (lower ISOs) have finer grains and can produce sharper images, but are less sensitive to light. In low light situations, a higher-speed film may be necessary.

Specific film types are not as important as are filters. Because the human eye and photographic film respond differently to colors, filters are added to alter the response of the film. For instance, our eyes see yellow as the brightest color, but film senses blue as the brightest. Filters enhance the contrasts in the sky and clouds and are vital for good work in weather photography. Basically they lighten objects of their own and similar colors, while darkening others. Some that are worthy to the job and their effects:

To Do: A comb nephoscope looks somewhat like a garden rake with its tines straight up. Its main portion is a 1-inch diameter rod about 8 feet long, with a 3-foot-long crosspiece spiked evenly with seven or eight half-inch dowels, each about 6 inches high. (Specific dimensions are not critical.) It is supported in such a way as to allow the rod to rotate. Its base has a pointer aligned with the crosspiece that indicates the compass directions on the base, which is oriented upon mounting.

To use the nephoscope, walk around it until you can view a particular cloud behind the center spike of the crosspiece. Twist the rod until the spikes of the crosspiece are aligned parallel to the direction of the cloud's motion. Read the compass direction on the base plate.

Filter	Advantage
Red	Renders blue sky nearly black; heightens dramatic effect.
Orange	Darkens sky, reduces distant haze; improves texture of sunlit objects.
Yellow	Mildly darkens the sky and brightens clouds.
Skylight	Reduces blue in shade or on heavily overcast days.
Polarizing	Darkens clear blue sky, enriches colors, cuts unwanted reflections and glare.
Ultraviolet/ Haze	Faithful to blue sky, captures cloud colors well; eliminates haze.

Photographing brightly lit clouds, rainbows, halos, coronas, and other colored optics can be both satisfying and, in the case of rare phenomena, scientifically significant. The thing to keep in mind about these is that they are essentially light sources, and if you depend on the camera's exposure meter, you may wind up with overexposures. If the sun is in the frame, cover it with another object in view, such as a leaf or street lamp or branch. Close the aperture one-half to one full stop more than the camera indicates, and make multiple exposures with varying f-stops.

Cloud Atlas. Keep a weather journal of observed cloud types, noting the various kinds appearing in one day, one week, one month. You may even wish to keep a "life list" as bird-watchers do, to document observance of all the clouds you have identified. Note the time and place as well as weather conditions at the time of observation. Sketch interesting clouds and their transmutations in the journal.

Bathroom Fog. Take a hot shower with the bathroom door closed and no exhaust fan on. Dew will form on the mirror, and a warming fog will permeate the room. Sing "Misty" real loud. Explain that you are testing sound travel in high humidity.

CHAPTER 5

Disturbances: Stormy Weather

Fair skies, despite their provision of beautiful sunsets and enjoyable weather, do not command the same amount of fascination as does stormy weather. Storms, being the squeaky wheels of the atmosphere, always generate the engaged attention of the innocent and interested victims of their fury: scientists and forecasters, farmers and outdoor workers, business owners and merchants, aviators and mariners, and nearly everyone else. Yet a storm's delivery of its products doesn't affect only humans and their immediate concerns, but the greater biosphere as a whole. All living inhabitants and natural resources are both unsettled and refreshed by the change in weather and the redistribution of air, water, heat, and pressure. This is the stuff of storms: the dynamic energy pitched about in association with low pressure areas, the results of the atmosphere being disturbed by solar radiation and forced over the rotating topography of the earth's crust.

Millions of small-scale circulations and turbulent motions throughout the world form and dissipate each minute. Though small, these weather events are not insignificant, because they are both caused by and influence larger-scale patterns. On the order of a few feet to a few dozen yards, and lasting mere seconds to several minutes, are the *microscale* phenomena. In this category are harmless small eddies and whirlwinds a few feet across that twirl dust and debris for a few seconds, but it also includes dangerous clear-air turbulence and thunderstorm microbursts that can slam an airplane to the ground and severe and highly damaging tornadoes and waterspouts that can last nearly an hour.

SCALES OF ATMOSPHERIC DISTURBANCES

	Approximate Size	Phenomena	Period
Microscale	6.5 ft (2 m)	Dust devil	seconds
	65 ft (20 m)	Waterspout, tornado	minutes
	650 ft (200 m)	Clear-air turbulence	
Mesoscale	1.25 mi (2 km)	Cumulus cloud	hours
	12.5 mi (20 km)	Large thunderstorm	
	125 mi (200 km)	Hurricane	days
Macroscale	1,250 mi (2000 km)	Midlatitude cyclone	week
	12,500 mi (20,000 km)	Long waves in westerlies	month

Medium-size *mesoscale* patterns on the order of 1.25 to 1,250 miles (roughly 2 to 2,000 kilometers) in size include towering cumulus and thunderstorms, the squall lines and gust fronts they spawn, circulations of land/sea and mountain/valley breezes, weather fronts, air pollution episodes, and severe weather outbreaks. This is the scale in which the Coriolis force becomes an important factor in their movements.

At a size over 1,250 miles (2,000 kilometers) are the longer-lasting *macroscale* events of midlatitude cyclones and anticyclones, jet streams, and large-scale troughs and ridges in the prevailing westerlies.

The weather at any particular location may be influenced by many interacting scales of motion, from the rogue dust devil to globe-girdling planetary waves. At any one time, a site may experience small-scale turbulence, convection, and a sea breeze, as well as the influence of the larger systems of weather fronts, a cyclone, and accompanying jet stream. It can be overwhelming at best, and confounding at worst, to try to understand all the forces and dynamics involved as a whole. Therefore we'll isolate certain disturbances and examine them individually to become better acquainted with the diversity, intensity, and peculiarities of weather's stormy portfolio.

FACT: Birds perch facing the wind.

TURBULENCE

Chaotic motions that fluctuate wildly in seemingly random and unpredictable ways are called *turbulence*. *Thermal turbulence* is the sort caused by the rising air columns of convection. When these thermals contain enough moisture, cumulus clouds form. *Mechanical turbulence* is formed in airstreams roughed up by rugged terrain. Both types are involved in everyday observations: the random shape of clouds as they evolve; smoke dispersed by the wind; steam billowing from a cooling tower; the unpredictability of weather patterns themselves—all exhibit the influence of turbulence in the environment.

Turbulence may be large or small, occur at any altitude, and be with or without clouds. Frequent small-scale eddies only a few inches in diameter form as chaotic swirls in the air, caused by a meeting of breezes from different directions. Such a little *dust whirl* can often be observed on city corners where winds along the streets meet at the intersections. Over a dry and dusty or sandy area, a rapidly rotating column of air may develop from strong convection during hot, sunny, and calm days. The *dust devil* picks up dust, leaves, dried cornstalks, and other light debris, may grow to several yards in diameter at the base, and rotate in either a clockwise or counterclockwise direction. The rotating column is not funnel-shaped like a tornado—nor is it attached to any cloud—but is wider at its base and top, and skinnier in the middle, rather like two cones with their apexes joined. The height is generally between 100 and 300 feet, but in a hot desert may even reach upwards of 2,000 feet. Its movement is slowly erratic during its life span of only a few minutes, as it makes its way to other patches of heated air.

Higher altitudes, with their low humidities and more frequent dramatic changes in wind shear, tend to produce clear-air turbulence. This is especially true near the wind-speed maximums that center along the jet streams. Encountered in flight, clear-air turbulence may make one feel like laundry applied to a washboard. On average, significant turbulence is encountered every other day on a commercial flight over the United States, sometimes severe enough to suddenly drop the plane as much as 200 feet, hurling flight attendants and food carts—and anything else not fastened down—to the ceiling. In December 1997, a jumbo jet over Japan plummeted several hundred feet in a matter of seconds in clear-air turbulence, killing one woman and injuring 102 other passengers.

Recent research has found that turbulence is composed not only of random movements, but also of an ordered, predictable form of eddying. This discovery may lead to a greater understanding of this hazardous marvel.

THUNDERSTORMS AND THEIR PROGENY

During the lifetime of a large cumulonimbus cloud and its kin, several different microscale storm events may be spawned by one severe mesoscale thunderstorm. To fully understand the relationships, causes, and effects, we'll take a look at the types of thunderstorms and how they grow, as well as their troublesome offspring.

> FACT: In the United States, average winds blow 10 to 25 mph two days a week—enough for the generation of wind-powered energy.

It is helpful to speak of a *cell* as one set of updrafts and downdrafts in a storm. Thunderstorms are categorized by the size and strength of their cells as single-cell, multicell cluster, multicell line, and supercell.

> FACT: To be classified as severe by the National Weather Service, a thunderstorm must produce at least one of the following: hail of three-quarter-inch diameter or greater; wind gusts 58 mph or greater; any size or duration of tornado.

Single-cell thunderstorm development begins with convective instability forming a cumulus cloud with its base at the lifting condensation level. If at that point, the air in the updraft remains sufficiently moist and warmer than its surroundings, the new cloud continues to grow upward, eventually becoming a towering cumulus. Ultimately, however, the rising air reaches a level at which its temperature is cooler than its surroundings, it is no longer buoyant, and it begins to sink. In larger storms, this does not happen until it reaches the warmer stratosphere, where temperature increases with height or remains constant.

The altitude at which the rising air's temperature matches that of its environment is appropriately called the equilibrium level. While the air at the top of the rising column is no longer buoyant, the updraft continues to pump air up to that level. As more and more arrives, it begins to spread horizontally, and further condensation forms the ice-filled anvil cloud, capping the towering cumulus and marking its transition to cumulonimbus.

Because this rising air can develop considerable momentum, it can also overshoot the equilibrium level and pierce the anvil with a "boiling-over" dome on the cloud. The amount of this overshoot, as measured by infrared satellite imagery, is used as an indicator of the degree of severity.

The mature stage of the thunderstorm begins when ice crystals and water droplets grow large enough to overcome the updraft and begin falling. The falling precipitation drags cooler air from the higher parts of the cloud into the lower, warmer section, producing downdrafts. The differences in temperature between the falling air and the rising air create stronger upward and downward motions, creating the storm's most violent stage.

> FACT: In severe weather, many birds will not leave their shelters to find food, because doing so would use more energy than what could be replaced by the food.

Single-cell Thunderstorm Life Cycle

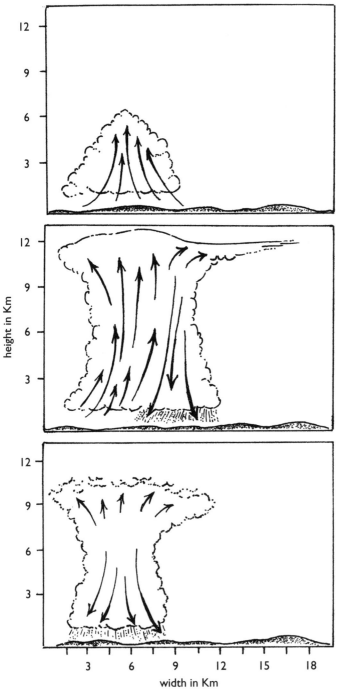

a. Growth Stage. Thermals rise and vapor condenses, forming a towering cumulus, with its base at the lifting condensation level.

b. Mature Stage. The top of the towering cumulus reaches the equilibrium level and spreads out. Ice particles form the anvil top. Falling precipitation creates down-drafts and more forceful vertical motions. Electrical charges build and separate; lightning is discharged.

c. Dissipating Stage. Downdrafts eventually bring enough cool dry air to the surface that the supply of warm moist air is diminished, updrafts cease, precipitation tapers off, and the storm dissipates.

Lightning. During the explosive growth stage of the thunderstorm and start of the precipitation, a static charge builds up within the cloud as ice crystals and water droplets grow, interact, and collide. It is believed that the smaller particles tend to accumulate a positive charge near the top of the cloud, while larger ones that fall acquire a more negative charge. Thus the upper part of the cumulonimbus takes on a strong positive charge; the lower part assumes a negative charge, which in turn induces a positive charge on the ground for several miles around the storm.

The voltage difference between areas of opposite charges can reach up to 7,500 volts over the distance of just one inch, and millions of volts over the entire cloud! Once the voltage difference exceeds the insulating capacity of the air, a lightning stroke occurs to complete the electrical circuit and discharge the buildup of static electricity, marking the official transformation from rain cloud to thunderstorm.

The first lightning flash of a thunderstorm is generally contained entirely within the cloud. A *luminous leader* traveling between charge centers initiates the discharge, and a lightning strike illuminates the interior of the storm for just two-tenths of a second. The charge is estimated to be a few thousand amperes.

Cloud-to-ground lightning flashes carry greater currents and each year kill as many as one hundred people, damage more than $40 million in property, and set over ten thousand fires consuming $50 million worth of marketable timber in the United States alone.

What our eyes see as a single stroke of cloud-to-ground lightning is usually several strokes in rapid succession, in both directions. The series begins as a *stepped leader* emerges from the thundercloud. Composed of luminous electrons, it moves in discrete steps of about 150 feet at a time, for just one-millionth of a second, pausing about fifty microseconds between steps, depositing a charge along a branching channel toward the ground. As it nears the ground, the stepped leader may draw a positively charged streamer upward, to intercept it and complete an ionized path to the ground. The cloud is then short-circuited and a brilliant return stroke flashes upward at about 60,000 miles per second, carrying 30,000 to 200,000 amps, peaking in just a few millionths of a second.

Such an instantaneous rise in current instantaneously heats the air in the lightning channel to temperatures exceeding 50,000°F. The heated air explosively expands, compressing the surrounding clear air, generating a shock wave that becomes an acoustic wave as it propagates away from the channel.

Lightning Stroke Sequence

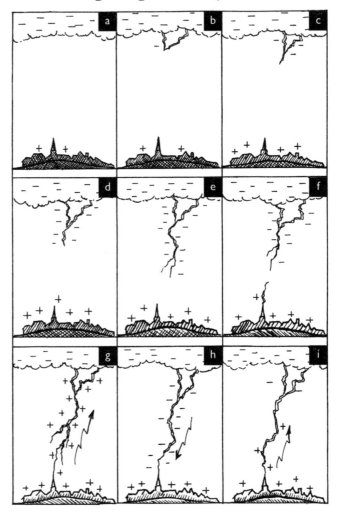

a. Positive charges accumulate near the top of the cloud; negative charges gather near the cloud's base, inducing a positive charge on the ground.

b. c. d. e. A stepped leader emerges from the cloud, carrying negative charges earthward, too fast for the eye to see.

f. A positively charged streamer from a tree or tall structure may form and meet the stepped leader, creating an ionized channel.

g. A brilliant ground-to-cloud return stroke flashes upward carrying positive charges; a shock wave is created from the extreme heating of the air in the channel.

h. A dart leader forms a cloud-to-ground strike following the same track downward without branching.

i. A second return stroke occurs upward. Dart leaders and return stroke exchanges may be repeated several times to constitute one lightning flash. Typical total stroke time elapsed: 30-300 microseconds. Typical total flash time elapsed: less than half a second.

The noise is thunder. Because sound travels relatively slowly, thunder heard as a sudden "crack" has been generated close by. Rumbling reverberations that follow may have actually been generated first, several miles away, at the start of the lightning stroke.

Upon completion of the first return stroke, small streamers occur in the cloud as precursors to the next stroke, followed by a luminous *dart leader* that emerges and follows the same track to the ground without branching, and a second stroke occurs. This is followed by another return stroke upward. Cloud-to-ground lightning flashes typically consist of three to four individual strokes, and at times as many as twenty or more, all in less than a second.

With the arrival of lightning, the thunderstorm has arrived, statistically speaking. A single-cell thunderstorm typically lasts twenty to thirty minutes and is capable of producing dangerous lightning and heavy rainfall. When convective conditions are favorable, a group of single-cell thunderstorms may merge and move as a unit, with each cell in a different stage of its life cycle. These *multicell cluster storms* are tempests ripe for even more violence, as they strengthen and assault the environs for an hour or longer.

FLASH-TO-BANG COUNTDOWN

Since light travels at 186,000 miles per second, the flash is seen the instant it occurs. Sound travels much more slowly—at about one-fifth of a mile per second. To estimate how far away the lightning stroke occurred, in miles, count the number of seconds between seeing the lightning flash and hearing the thunder, and divide by five.

If the count is 10 to 15 seconds, meaning the flash was 2 to 3 miles away, seek shelter. Successive lightning strokes can be 2 to 3 miles apart, and you could be the next target. Don't be lulled into complacency that the storm is still a ways off. Lightning has been known to leap through clear air to strike several miles away from the storm, in what is the proverbial "bolt from the blue." Remember the 30-30 Rule: When you see lightning, count the seconds until you hear thunder. If that is 30 seconds or less, you're in the danger zone; seek shelter. Wait for 30 minutes since the last lightning strike before going back out.

FACT: About 100,000 thunderstorms occur in the United States annually. An estimated two thousand are in progress at this very moment throughout the world, producing some one hundred flashes per second.

THE MANY FACES OF LIGHTNING

Forked. Typical cloud-to-ground lightning, also called *streak* lightning.

Sheet. Intracloud flash in which no branches of the stroke are visible.

Heat. Cloud-to-ground flash seen from a distance; no thunder is heard; appears red or orange.

Ribbon. Rare form of cloud-to-ground lightning that occurs in strong wind blowing perpendicular to the line of sight, spreading the channel sideways as successive strokes follow in it, widening the observed flash.

Bead. Cloud-to-ground lightning in which some sections of the channel remain luminous longer than others; also called *pearl* or *chain* lightning.

Ball. Extremely rare, luminous ball of light 1 to 3 feet in diameter that may move rapidly among objects or float through the air. It is usually preceded by a lightning flash, and lasts a few seconds to a few minutes. Accompanied by hissing noise, it may explode or disappear noiselessly. Although observed and reported, it has not been proven scientifically.

St. Elmo's fire. A luminous greenish or bluish glow above pointy objects at the surface. First observed on ship masts, and named for the patron saint of sailors, it is caused by the soft glow of an electrical field as positive charges stream skyward toward negative charges in the cloud. Technically called a *corona discharge.*

Red sprites, blue jets, green elves. Recently discovered, distinctively shaped colored flashes, discharging from the tops of thunderstorms into high altitudes above; occur at the same time as discharges within the cloud.

SYMBOLS FOR STORMY WEATHER

$\Bigl\langle$ ↓ lightning	T thunder	↗ St. Elmo's fire
⏦ polar aurora	℞ thunderstorm	℞ severe thunderstorm
●/✳︎ ℞ thunderstorm with rain and/or snow	△ ℞ severe thunderstorm with hail	∇ squall
	)(funnel cloud	

'MAY LIGHTNING STRIKE ME IF . . .'

The top six most common activities associated with lightning strikes:

  6. Using or repairing electrical appliances.
  5. Using the telephone.
  4. Playing golf.
  3. Working on heavy farm or construction equipment.
  2. Boating, fishing, swimming.
  1. Being out in an open field.

LIGHTNING SAFETY

The following lifesaving tips are from the National Weather Service disaster preparedness program.

Don't seek shelter under a lone tree. Isolated trees, especially tall ones, make very effective lightning rods and attract lightning. Standing under trees is probably the deadliest thing you can do in a thunderstorm.

Do go indoors, if at all possible. Most lightning deaths and injuries occur outdoors. Indoor casualties are rare and come mostly from being in contact with electrical appliances and plumbing fixtures, or from lightning-caused fires.

Don't be the highest object around. If you're unable to go indoors, don't stand on a hilltop, in an open field, or on a boat.

Do plan ahead. Get the latest weather information on NOAA weather radio. Listen for static on your AM radio. Keep a sharp weather eye. Give yourself time to get to safety.

Don't stay in the water. Get out, regardless of whether it's a swimming pool, lake, or ocean. Get off the beaches.

Do get off of and away from farm and construction equipment, unless it has an enclosed metal cab. Get off of and away from motorcycles and bicycles, too.

Don't be near wire fences, metal plumbing, railings, and other metallic paths that might conduct electricity to you from a distance.

Don't use golf clubs, aluminum tennis rackets, or other metal objects when thunderstorms threaten. Get to safety.

Do spread out. Groups caught in a thunderstorm should split up. That way, if lightning strikes the group, the least possible number will be affected.

As a last resort: Suppose you're unable to go indoors or seek other appropriate shelter. You find yourself hopelessly isolated in a level field. Suddenly you feel your hair standing on end—indicating your body is taking on a strong electrical charge. It means you're about the become a lightning target. *Immediately drop to your knees and bend forward, with your hands on your knees.* This will not necessarily prevent your being struck, but it's the best compromise between keeping a low profile and minimizing the flow of current between you and the ground. You *can* survive lightning. About two-thirds of lightning victims fully recover.

THE DEADLY MYTHS OF LIGHTNING

Deadly Myth #1

Lightning never strikes the same place twice. Wrong! If a spot is exposed and vulnerable, it is very likely to be struck frequently. "Taking the path of least resistance" also means that lightning is actually more likely to strike in the same place more than once, since the channel is already warmed and conducive to a lightning stroke.

Deadly Myth #2

Rubber-soled shoes protect you from lightning. Think of it: a giant spark travels miles through the air, carrying several thousand amps, to be stopped by a half-inch of rubber? Wrong!

(Possibly) Deadly Myth #3

The car is the safest place to be in a thunderstorm. Not necessarily. Assuming we're not talking about a convertible, a car is relatively safe because the metal body of the car would conduct the electrical current of a strike around you to the ground, *provided you're not touching anything metal inside the car.* The rubber tires do not insulate the car. A safer place to be during a thunderstorm is in a strongly constructed building installed with lightning rods.

Hail. At the cloud top where individual ice crystals may remain for a time in an area of supercooled water droplets, an ice pellet will grow as water droplets strike the ice and freeze on contact. This hailstone, in order to survive melting as it falls through the cloud and to the ground, must remain for at least a few minutes in the presence of supercooled water. This in turn requires updrafts strong enough to counteract the terminal fall velocity of the hailstone, typically 10 to 40 mph. Most thunderstorms do not develop such strong updrafts, and that is why hail that reaches the ground is relatively uncommon.

In more severe storms, updrafts can easily suspend the hailstone above the melting level for long periods. When this happens, hail will grow until it is too heavy, or is heaved into a part of the cloud where the updrafts are weak, and it makes a hasty exit to the ground. Because the thunderstorm is usually on the move, hail is typically deposited in a swath 10 to 15 miles wide and up to 100 miles long.

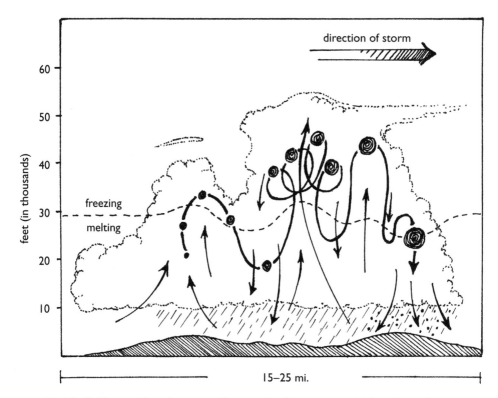

Multicell Cluster Thunderstorm Showing Hail Formation. *Multicells are the most common variety of thunderstorms, in which individual cells, clustered and moving as one cloud, exist at varying stages of growth, maturity, and dissipation. Varying strengths of updrafts and downdrafts, which also progress forward as the storm advances, provide the means for hailstone growth, and account for the varying intensities and amounts of rainfall measured at points along the surface track.*

In the varying stages of a multicell cluster storm, stronger, wetter updrafts of the more mature cells coexist next to younger, dryer, and weaker updrafts. As the storm advances and a hail embryo grows, it rides a looping roller-coaster trip through varying-strength updrafts and downdrafts, rising and falling several times past the freezing/melting level and through varying concentrations and sizes of cloud droplets.

Partial melting occurs in the warm parts of the cluster, and freezing in the cold parts, producing a multilayered hailstone of varying textures and appearances, formed by alternate layers of glaze and rime. As it grows in size, a roughly spherical shape may give way to a conical or irregular cluster of smaller stones clumped together. Eventually, the stone's weight can no longer be supported, and the cloud starts spitting ice.

THAT'S ABOUT THE SIZE OF IT

It's fortunate that common knowledge includes many different sizes of spheroids. How else could we describe hail sizes? Pea-sized hail may have been quite a bit larger before its fall. Marble-sized hail is about the average size from Midwest storms and can dent a car roof. Golf-ball-sized hail can destroy a corn crop. Hardball-sized and grapefruit-sized can maim and kill livestock and people.

The largest recorded hailstone in the United States was an icy monster with a 17.5-inch girth, that fell on Coffeyville, Kansas, on September 3, 1979. In its longest dimension, it measured 5.7 inches wide, and was calculated to have had a terminal fall velocity of 105 mph. A one-and-a-half pounder, measuring 17 inches in circumference, fell on Potter, Nebraska, on July 6, 1928.

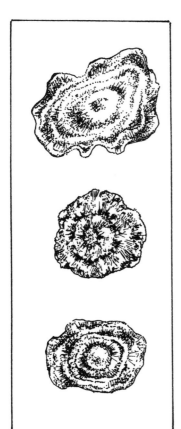

Cross Sections of Hailstones.
The concentric pattern is formed
by alternating layers of rime and
glaze as the hailstone revisits
both sides of the freezing/melting
level in its ride through the
thunderstorm.

Squall Line and Gust Front. *The* squall line *consists of several multicell storms organized into a row and moving as one unit. A coordinated series of downdrafts along its leading edge may develop a* gust front *of high winds and sharp difference in temperature.*

Squall Lines and Gust Fronts. Cumulonimbus, like smaller clouds, have a tendency to align themselves into lines, which reduce their overall surface area vulnerable to evaporation. A *multicell line storm,* or *squall line,* consists of a continuous row of thunderstorms that may extend hundreds of miles. Unlike isolated storms, these menaces are frequently associated with larger-scale motions and are often harbingers of a rapidly advancing cold front. Squall lines are usually in a hurry to move eastward, and they persist for several hours.

FACT: A thunderstorm with a diameter of 3 miles may contain 500,000 tons of water.

A characteristic feature of a squall line is a well-developed *gust front* at its leading edge, formed from a series of downdrafts. This cold, dry air originated some 1.5 to 4 miles up, where frozen and liquid precipitation fell through it, melting and evaporating as it went, thereby cooling it and making it denser and heavier than the surrounding air. Falling to the ground and spreading laterally, it forcibly displaces the warmer air at the surface.

If the motion of the warmer air is contrary to the direction of the newly arrived cold air, a gust front forms. Its passage is marked by strong, gusty winds and a sharp temperature drop—as much as 15°F in a few seconds.

The gust front displays a distinctive *shelf cloud* along its leading edge. When viewed front-on, it appears as an ominous, smooth black shelf sloping up and back toward the storm, almost like a huge, old-time locomotive cowcatcher, extending from horizon to horizon at a low altitude. When viewed from behind, its fierce internal turbulence is on display, eerily backlit and sinister.

The shelf cloud forms within the warm layer being force-fed into the updrafts of the convection cells by the cold downdrafts. As the warm air is lifted, it all becomes saturated at the same altitude, forming the uniform base of the cloud, and propelling the storm's growth and advance.

The forward speed of the gust front depends on the temperature difference between the cold and warm air, the depth of the cold air, and the speed of the warm air, but typically ranges from 20 to 45 mph. In some cases the gust front can exceed 50 mph and sustain damaging winds. Should the speed of the gust front outrace the thundercloud itself, the convection machine of the storm suddenly finds itself cut off from its source of buoyant air, with only rain-cooled, dense air beneath it, and sees the start of the dissipating stage: the beginning of the end of the storm.

If the warm air at the ground moves so rapidly toward and into the thunderstorm that the gust front can make no headway against it, a different danger arises. Such strong convection stalls the forward momentum of the storm, and it may simply "camp out" for a while in one location, bringing a steady downpour and causing flash flooding.

IN A FLASH

Flash floods can move with incredible speed, tearing out trees, washing away roads, destroying buildings and bridges, and scouring new channels. Advance warnings are not always possible; take precautions when a watch is issued. When a flash flood warning is issued, act immediately; there may only be seconds to save your life.

Get to higher ground immediately.

Get out of areas subject to flooding: dips, low spots, canyons, swales, and so forth.

Avoid already flooded areas. Do not attempt to cross a flowing stream where the water is above your knee.

Do not drive through flooded areas. Shallow, swiftly flowing water can wash a car from the roadway, which may not even be intact under the water.

Abandon a stalled vehicle immediately and seek higher ground. Rapidly rising water may engulf the vehicle and sweep it and its passengers away.

Downbursts and Microbursts. The downdrafts in a thunderstorm sometimes gain such momentum and force that they plummet right out of the bottom of the storm and smash on the ground. This downward vigor can be so strong that when it hits the ground and spreads horizontally, it is capable of tornado-force winds, but is no tornado. Called a *downburst*, it is generally directed toward the front of the storm, where it contributes to the storm's forward momentum.

At times a downburst may concentrate damaging winds in excess of 150 mph to an area no larger than 2.5 miles across. Such *microbursts* are the more probable culprits in many storm damages blamed on tornadoes, especially in cases where victims have not seen or heard a funnel cloud. Unlike tornadoes, which scour circular or semicircular swaths, microbursts leave a tell-tale starburst pattern of radiating damage away from ground zero. Not identified until the mid-1970s, microbursts have since been linked to several aircraft crashes. Most microbursts last only a few minutes, but some have lasted as long as half an hour.

Derecho. An especially large and windy squall line that creates a series of downbursts as it races along is called a *derecho* (pronounced day-RAY-cho; from the Spanish, meaning "straight ahead" or "direct"). Derechos produce damaging straight-line winds (not associated with any rotation) in excess of 58 mph, over areas hundreds of miles long and more than 100 miles across. They are especially common to the Midwest in late spring and into summer.

Firestorm. Microbursts, with their tremendous surges of oxygen, can transform small wildfires into major conflagrations. Large wildfires, in turn, can create their own circulations of rotating rising air, as the extreme heating leads to highly unstable conditions. If the convective column generates its own inflow, a firestorm is born, and the resultant cloud even gets its own name: *pyrocumulus.* With winds fierce enough to uproot trees and break limbs, the storm multiplies the peril by scattering burning embers for miles around, setting new fires.

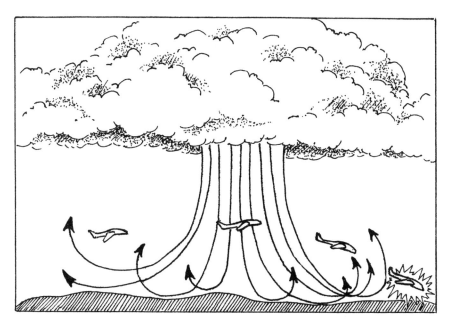

Microbursts. Because microbursts are very small, and may or may not be marked by rainfall, they are difficult for a pilot to spot, and even harder to respond to quickly enough if caught in one. As a low-flying plane enters a microburst, the plane suddenly has a strong headwind, which is fine for flying. But as the plane proceeds through it, the head wind rapidly shifts to a tailwind, which suddenly and dramatically cuts the amount of lift generated by the wings. The plane may crash before it is able to regain enough speed to create the necessary lift.

A WHO'S WHO OF
THUNDERSTORM HAZARDS

Derecho. Severe straight-line winds that may damage over 10,000 square miles during one episode.

Downburst and microburst. Damaging winds up to 150 mph that destroy property and present sudden dangers to aircraft.

Firestorm. Surging winds that fan wildfires into raging infernos.

Flash Flood. Suddenly rising waters from excessive precipitation; kills an average of 150 people in the United States each year.

Gust front. Terrific wind shear and temperature gradients, making them the sharpest boundaries in the atmosphere.

Gustnado. Eddy in the gust front; adds rotating winds and their damages to the straight-wind blasts.

Hail. Responsible for annual U.S. property and crop damages in the hundreds of millions of dollars.

Lightning. Kills 75 to 100 people in the United States annually; electrocutes cattle, explodes trees, sets fires, destroys electrical equipment.

Tornado. Extremely destructive rotating winds; kills an average of forty-eight Americans per year.

Waterspout. Presents special dangers to boaters and shore properties; likely participant in so-called Bermuda Triangle incidents.

SEVERE WEATHER WORDS

These advisories are issued exclusively by the National Weather Service, and are coupled with an announcement of what type of hazard exists (severe thunderstorm warning, tornado watch, etc.).

Watch: The hazard is possible. Conditions are more favorable for its occurrence than usual. The watch recommends planning, preparation, and increasing awareness.

Warning: The hazard exists. It is either imminent or has been reported. The warning indicates the need for action to protect life and property.

Supercell Thunderstorms. As nasty as a squall line can be with its arsenal of downpours, lightning, hail, gust front, and microbursts, it can get worse. The granddaddy thunderstorm of all is one in which everything is more intense: heavier precipitation, more dangerous lightning, larger hail, higher wind gusts, greater potential for greater numbers of microbursts, and, lest we forget, greater outbreaks of tornadoes.

Such large and long-lasting thunderstorms are known as *supercells,* in which updrafts can approach an unbelievable 170 mph! In the presence and right combination of strong wind shear, updrafts 2 to 6 miles in diameter twist in the wind as they rise, forming a column of air called a *mesocyclone,* rotating at a speed of 50 mph or more. This becomes the difference between "the men and the boys" of thunderstorm activity.

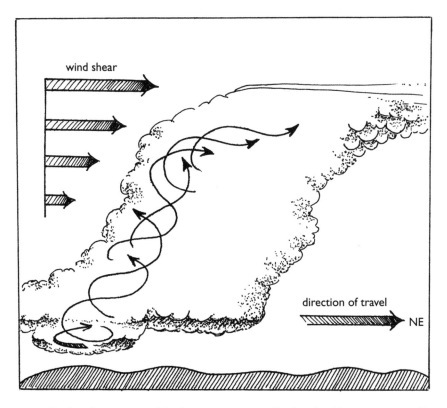

Supercell Thunderstorm. Unlike the varying-stage cells of multicell storms, supercells organize just one or two that create a rotating mesocyclone core. A vertical wind shear tilts the cloud and its spiraling center toward the northeast, which prohibits precipitation and downdrafts from interfering with the rising air racing to the top of the troposphere. A rotating wall cloud may drop out of the rear flank minutes before a tornado appears.

Unlike the up and down pulses of other thunderstorms, supercells organize just one or two cells, each with its own steadily maintained updraft and coexisting—but noninterfering—downdraft, fueling and intensifying the storm. The mesocyclone core, tilted toward the northeast by the wind shear, prevents hail and rain from falling back down into the rising air. Instead, precipitation falling out of the tilted updraft evaporates in the dry, midlevel air on the northeast side of the supercell, causing this air to cool and fall to the earth.

In lesser thunderclouds, precipitation falling into the rising air dampens the upward momentum, and the storm slits its own throat, so to speak, cutting off its lifeblood of buoyant air and dissipating in thirty minutes or so. But the supercell, with its unique internal circulation system, can sustain an intense terrorizing spree for several hours over hundreds of miles.

Tornado! I don't think it's possible to say that word without an exclamation point! No man-made structure is able to take a direct hit by a strong tornado. A twisting vortex of winds that can exceed 300 mph, the tornado in action is one of nature's most awesome—and humbling—displays of power.

All categories of thunderstorms can generate tornadoes. In smaller, non-supercell thunderstorms, a weak tornado can form in the gust front of the storm, without the characteristic condensation of a funnel cloud attached to a parent cloud, and is sometimes called a *gustnado*. Its formation is similar to that of a small eddy that swirls in a fast-flowing stream as it pours around an object. With a shallow vortex, gustnadoes generally last less than five minutes and rarely exceed 150 mph.

The potential for tornadoes is greatest in the supercell thunderstorm, which is more likely to develop during springtime in the Midwest, although they can and do form at all times of the year. Prime supercell habitat is found where a mile-deep layer of warm, moist air at the surface is overlaid with cool, dry air. A vertical wind shear penetrates both air masses. Separating them is a thin, stable temperature inversion, which serves as a lid to the inherent stability.

If the low-level air can be forced upward to break through the inversion layer, runaway convection results in the highly unstable environment. This may occur through one or more common means: The sun heats the surface, generating thermals; jet streams and upper-level disturbances cause low-level convergence; or the frontal systems of an invading cyclone force-lifts it.

Such mixing produces perfect conditions for the development of surface low pressure and growth of supercells along the frontal boundaries. The formation of a rotating mesocyclone further intensifies the low at the surface, and rapid, fierce convergence of low-level air streams toward the center of the updraft.

Just as the spin of an ice-skater increases as his arms pull inward—due to conservation of angular momentum—a 40 mph wind flowing around the low pressure area at a distance of 5 miles from its center can escalate considerably when reined in to a radius of 1 mile. As the low pressure dramatically deepens, the air at the center expands and cools below its dew point, producing the ominous funnel cloud of the tornado.

FACT: On April 3–4, 1974, 127 tornadoes tracked across the central United States, in Mississippi, Alabama, Georgia, Tennessee, North Carolina, Kentucky, West Virginia, Virginia, Illinois, Indiana, Ohio, Michigan, and New York. A total of 315 people were killed, 6,142 were injured, and 27,590 families shared property losses estimated at more than $600 million.

The exact process by which tornadoes form is still not clearly understood. Doppler radar shows that the funnel cloud first forms in the midlevels of the cloud, then extends both upward into the storm's higher levels and downward to the ground. But the tornado can exist on the ground without a visible cloud and still inflict calamity.

Sometimes its presence is first noted by a column of swirling debris before the funnel cloud condenses. Sometimes the vortex itself is hidden by surrounding clouds, precipitation, flying dust and debris, hills, trees, or buildings.

WINDOW-STRESSING

Higher pressure inside a structure is swiftly and powerfully obliged to seek a tornado's lower pressure outside, which may be as much as 10 percent lower. Such a difference on a windowpane loads 700 more pounds of pressure per square foot on the inside than on the outside, literally exploding windows outward. Still, most damage results from the high winds, rather than from pressure differences, and windows are often blown out and broken from flying debris even before the funnel cloud arrives.

FUJITA WIND-DAMAGE SCALE

Developed by tornado researcher T. Theodore Fujita in the late 1960s, the Fujita Scale corre-lates the extent of storm damage to wind speed. Although the descriptive words are obviously inadequate, the categories are useful for research and identification purposes. Damage up to F-3 is capable from a microburst. A category of F-6, from 319 mph to Mach 1, the speed of sound, is not believed to be physically possible. If it were, it might have to be described as "inconceivable."

Category	Wind (mph)	Approx. Frequency	Approx. Lifespan	Description	Interpretation
F-0 weak	40–72	29%	<10 min.	Light	Chimney damage, tree branches broken
F-1 weak	73–112	40%	<10 min.	Moderate	Mobile homes pushed or overturned
F-2 strong	113–157	24%	<20 min.	Considerable	Trees uprooted, mobile homes demolished
F-3 strong	158–206	6%	<20 min.	Severe	Roofs and walls torn down, cars thrown, trains overturned
F-4 violent	207–260	2%	<60 min.	Devastating	Well-constructed walls demolished
F-5 violent	261–318	<1%	60 min.	Incredible	Homes lifted off foundations and carried away; cars airborne for 100 yards or more

The funnel may appear black from the load of debris it carries, white from the condensed water vapor, or take on the color of the dust it sucks up. It may look like a vast rotating cloud on the ground, or as a narrow rope extending 1,000 feet into the sky. As it dissipates, it may contort and become nearly horizontal in its stretched connection to the ground.

THE TORNADO'S APPOINTMENT BOOK

Motto: Always in Season!

Peak Occurrence Calendar

    Southeast states: December–March

    Central states: March–May

    Northern Tier and Southwest states: July–September

Preferred Touchdown Appointments: 3 P.M.–6 P.M.

Least Favored Performance Times: 5 A.M.–6 A.M.

Usual Direction of Approach: Southwest to Northeast

Range of Forward Speed: 0–70 mph, average 30 mph

Favored Unpredictability Tricks: skipping, hopping, jumping, turning

---

About 98 percent of all tornadoes have winds of less than 200 mph and last for just a few minutes, with typical damage paths about 150 feet wide and 9 miles long. The fraction that exceed that level, however, account for about 70 percent of all tornado deaths, and may cut up to a mile wide and 200 miles long.

Damage on the ground often exhibits a capricious and malefic nature: utter devastation sprinkled with fully unscathed swatches. The destruction is primarily caused by the high winds, not by the extreme low pressure, as was once thought. Roofs are commonly lifted by gusts of under 100 mph, and ceilings and walls are forced upward and outward by wind entering broken windows and blown-in doors. Trees are pulled out of the ground by their roots; railroad cars and mobile homes may be tossed about like empty soda cans. The landscape can be swept completely clean, and houses pared to their slab foundations. Pieces of debris, large and small, become missiles in the fantastic wind, to impale themselves in anything not yet moving. An unmistakable, earsplitting clamor, likened to that of a thousand freight trains, narrates the maelstrom.

Most tornadoes consist of a single column rotating cyclonically, but some are accompanied by a pair or more of smaller condensation funnels or debris clouds called *suction vortices* revolving around a common center, scouring their own swirls of damage about the main swath. Such an arrangement is called a *multi-vortex tornado.*

The largest, longest-lasting, and most damaging tornadoes are spawned in the rain-free area of a supercell, under a low, cyclonically rotating *wall cloud.*

TORNADO SAFETY

Advance Preparations:

Prepare disaster supplies, and store for portability in a backpack or dufflebag. Include flashlight and extra batteries, portable battery-operated radio with weather band, first-aid kit, emergency food and water, non-electric can opener, essential medicines, cash and credit cards, and sturdy shoes.

Develop an emergency communication and reuniting plan for family members. Long distance phone service usually remains intact even if local service is out. Arrange for everyone to check in with an out-of-state contact.

Learn basic first-aid and CPR; know how to turn off gas, electric, and water supplies.

When inside a building:

Go immediately to the lowest level of the building. If there is no basement or cellar, go to an inner hallway, bathroom, or closet without windows.

Avoid rooms with wide-span roofs, such as auditoriums, cafeterias, large hallways, enclosed malls. Smaller rooms afford greater protection from their walls than do large rooms.

Get away from windows. Do not take the time to open them. Open windows do not measurably help to equalize pressure, but do allow damaging winds to enter the building and push the roof upward and the walls outward.

Stay in the center of the room; corners are where debris collects.

Get under sturdy furniture, such as a table or workbench, and hold on to it. If in a bathroom, lie down in the tub and hold a mattress over you for protection from flying debris.

Abandon a mobile home for more secure shelter.

When in a vehicle:

Never try to outdrive a tornado. Tornadoes often change direction quickly and can toss cars and trucks through the air.

Abandon the car immediately and take shelter in a nearby building.

When outdoors:

Get inside a building if at all possible.

Lie in a ditch or low-lying area, or crouch near a strong building, if shelter is not available. Be aware of the potential for flooding.

Always use your arms to protect your head and neck, no matter where you are.

Multi-vortex Tornado. *An especially violent tornado may have accomplices revolving about it. These suction vortices can create even stronger winds at the ground, but generally do not last as long as the main twister.*

Formed by an abrupt lowering of the storm's base, wall clouds are persistently localized at the rear (south – southwest) edge of the storm, where humid, rain-cooled air is ingested into the updraft. With a diameter of a few thousand feet up to 5 miles, wall clouds usually develop a few minutes to an hour before spinning off a violent tornado. The lifespan of these tornadoes may be twenty to thirty minutes or longer as they touch down, disappear, and reappear sporadically and erratically along the travel path of the thunderstorm.

Waterspout. Should a tornado move over open water, it becomes known as a *waterspout,* and can do just as much damage to properties on and near the water. But most true waterspouts that form entirely over water are not as big or as intense as their land-based kin: maybe 150 feet wide, with wind speeds of 50 mph.

Like a tornado, the visible cloud of a waterspout is composed of water droplets, not water that's been sucked up from the surface. Unlike a tornado,

U.S. Annual Average Number of Tornadoes, 1950–1995

however, a waterspout often forms in relatively fair weather, attached to towering cumulus that may have reached only 8,000 feet—not even high enough to freeze at its top. By comparison, the supercells of land-based tornadoes may extend to greater than 50,000 feet high, and well into the freezing zone.

Waterspouts are more common than tornadoes, especially over warm, shallow water; the Florida Keys sees nearly one hundred waterspouts per month during the summer, and up to five hundred a year. The high water surface temperatures and high humidities in the lowest 2,000 feet of the air favors such frequent development. This unstable condition is very similar to that produced in strongly heated deserts, making waterspouts more closely related to dust devils than to true tornadoes.

OBSERVATIONS AND ACTIVITIES

Updrafts and Falling Velocities. You can mimic an updraft that keeps raindrops or hailstones suspended.

Materials: Electric hair dryer, Ping Pong ball, Nerf ball, tennis ball.

To Know: Updrafts in a cumulus cloud may rise at speeds of 15 to 30 feet per second, but may reach speeds of 125 to 200 feet per second, keeping raindrops and hailstones suspended in the air. As the raindrops or hailstones grow, they may eventually become too heavy to be supported by the updraft, and they fall out of the cloud. They reach terminal falling velocities according to their sizes, shapes, and weights.

To Do: Turn on the hair dryer and point it upward. Place the Ping Pong ball in its airstream. It will remain suspended in the flow. If the hair dryer has different speeds, try each one. Turn off the hair dryer, representing a cutoff in updraft. Try again with the Nerf ball and the tennis ball. If the Nerf ball is too light, soak it in water and try again. What can you deduce about the sizes and weights of cloud droplets, raindrops, hailstones, and updrafts? From a second-floor window, simultaneously drop all three balls. How does size, weight, density, and air resistance affect falling velocities?

Don't Give Me That Static. You can get a charge out of some home-grown lightning made with static electricity.

Materials: Plastic comb, piece of wool or fur, metal doorknob, balloons, black pepper, puffed rice, plate, bowl, water, yardstick, two chairs, carpeted floor.

To Know: When plastic and wool are rubbed together, atoms in the plastic pick up electrons from the wool, leaving the wool with an overall positive charge and the plastic with an overall negative charge. Should the charge difference build up, electrons will suddenly "jump" to equalize the charges. This motion makes the air hot, causing a spark. Lightning is a giant spark caused by the discharge of static electricity, as positive and negative electrical charges separate, build up, then suddenly jump from one location to another. It may occur between portions of the same cloud, from cloud to cloud, from cloud to ground, and from ground to cloud. Tiny sparks of static electricity mimic lightning strokes, but are harmless and easy to generate.

To Do: These experiments work best in dry air.

1. Rub the plastic comb with the piece of wool to charge the comb. Hold the comb near the metal doorknob and observe the spark it generates. Charge the comb again and insert it into a bowl of dry puffed rice; grains of rice stick

to the comb. Bring the charged comb near a thin stream of water from a faucet; note how it deflects the flow.

2. Inflate a balloon and charge it by rubbing it against your hair; observe yourself in the mirror as you hold the balloon near your hair. Charge the balloon again with your hair or the wool and hold it over some pepper sprinkled on a plate. What happens? Add water to the plate and float some pepper on its surface. Bring the charged balloon near the water. What happens now?

3. Hang two inflated balloons side by side from a yardstick suspended between two chairs. Rub one with the wool. How do the balloons react? Rub both balloons to charge them equally: now what happens? Note that identical static electric charges repel each other; opposites attract.

4. Take off your shoes and shuffle across a carpeted room in your socks. Touch the doorknob or other metal object to discharge the static electricity that accumulated in your body. Try discharging it to someone else.

5. Go into a darkened room and repeat the sock-shuffle shock experiment to better see the spark. Blow up two balloons, charge them with the wool, and touch them together in the dark. Observe your mini-lightning strikes. Pop the balloons to create thunder.

Dissect a Hailstone. Splitting open a hailstone's interior reveals its formation of concentric layers of ice.

Materials: Hailstones, tape measure, ruler, postal scale, newspaper, hammer, chisel, paper, pencil.

To Know: The concentric rings of a hailstone give an indication of the number of times the hailstone crossed the freezing/melting level in the thunderstorm. Alternate layers of rime and glaze create the pattern.

To Do: Collect hailstone specimens as soon as possible after they've landed. Measure and record the diameters, circumferences, and weights, as well as the date, time, and location collected. Spread them on the newspaper and use the hammer and chisel to split them apart. Count the number of rings. Make sketches of them.

Create and Observe a Mini-microburst. On a day cold enough to see your breath, forcefully exhale on a convenient cold and flat surface, such as the side of a car, and watch the swirl of the air after it slams into the obstruction. Repeat it many times to compare the speed and amount of your exhalation to the eventual extent of your breath-burst. Demonstrate it for onlookers. Explain that you're just making severe weather.

CHAPTER 6

Cyclones: Lows on the Go

"This room looks like a cyclone hit it!"

Did you grow up hearing this declaration from your mother? I did. And because of that I thought cyclones were pretty much the ultimate in devastation, somewhere between "beyond redemption" and "grounded for the rest of your life."

Generally speaking, cyclones are simply any low pressure area, no matter what size, and include dust devils, tornadoes, and mesocylones, as well as hurricanes and larger, land-based macroscale cyclones. All exhibit a counterclockwise rotation in the northern hemisphere (clockwise in the southern hemisphere) and are purveyors of unsettled weather. In their greatest manifestations, well-developed and intense macroscale cyclones are capable of map-altering erosion, dam-busting floods, town-burying blizzards, property-pummeling precipitation, and life-threatening conditions: fearful devastations all.

Because of such a broad definition, the term cyclone has come to mean different things to different people. To some, it means a tornado as they head to the cyclone cellar; on the Atlantic coast of the United States, it refers to a hurricane; to the TV weather reporter, it means a low pressure synoptic storm; to my mom it means a huge mess. In this chapter, we'll examine two of its common variations: the water-based formation of the *tropical cyclone,* and the land-based storm system known as the *midlatitude cyclone* (especially in its form as a creator of snowstorms).

Midlatitude cyclones are low pressure storms associated with cold, warm, and occluded fronts, that primarily get their energy from horizontal temperature gradients. Tropical cyclones live off the energy derived from the evaporation of warm seawater in the presence of high winds and lowered pressure, and the condensation of its convective thermals.

Midlatitude cyclones have cores cooler than their surroundings (cold core) and their strongest winds near the tropopause; tropical cyclones have warm cores with their strongest winds at the surface.

TROPICAL CYCLONES

A tropical cyclone is a mesoscale storm of 125 to 1,250 miles in diameter, formed over warm water whose evaporation is the source of energy. Tropical cyclones with sustained winds under 39 mph are called *tropical depressions;* those with winds 39 to 73 mph are known as *tropical storms* in the North Atlantic and North Pacific. Those with winds at or exceeding 74 miles per hour are called *hurricanes* in the North Atlantic and eastern North Pacific, and *typhoons* in the western North Pacific. Elsewhere, the generic term of tropical cyclone is used.

Tropical depressions and storms generally originate near the Cape Verde Islands off the western coast of Africa from a kink in the normally straight, easterly flow of surface air, called a *tropical wave*. These disturbances, also known as African easterly waves, are believed to be generated by instabilities in the Africa jet stream produced by the temperature contrast between the hot Sahara desert and the cooler temperatures along the Gulf of Guinea coast. These westward-moving waves are low pressure troughs of enhanced convection with a wavelength of 1,250 to 1,750 miles and a period of three to four days.

Some sixty of these surface air waves are generated over North Africa every year; most do not develop any further. Most of those that do continue developing reach only the depression or the storm stage.

The hurricane—a tropical cyclone to the max—is a relatively rare beast: fewer than 10 percent of all tropical disturbances. However, nearly 85 percent of severe hurricanes have their origins in these surface air waves. It has been suggested that possibly all the tropical cyclones that occur in the eastern Pacific can trace their beginnings back to Africa.

Favorable conditions for further development require a set of simultaneous circumstances. In addition to warm ocean water of at least 80°F, the atmosphere over the warm water must cool fast enough with height so that it is potentially unstable for moist convection. Relatively moist layers in the mid-troposphere assist continuing upward development. At the top of the troposphere, an upper-level high pressure area helps pump away air rising in the storm. Little or no vertical wind shear avoids disrupting the organization of tall convective cells. Should all these conditions be met, yet be within 300 miles, or 2 degrees latitude, of the equator, a tropical cyclone will still not form. It needs to be far enough away from the equator to be influenced by the Coriolis force to maintain the low pressure.

Given favor and time, a young disturbance may reach the second stage of development when low-level winds remain less than 39 mph, but the circulation closes, and the storm becomes a tropical depression.

The third stage begins when sustained winds reach 39 mph, and the now-tropical storm is given a name. The name is useful in tracking the storm as it moves, and as it possibly develops to hurricane strength with 74 mph winds and circularly symmetric spiral bands of clouds and intense rainfall.

Some eighty tropical cyclones thrive in the favored areas of the world each year. Of these, about one-third to one-half achieve hurricane status. In the northern hemisphere, these convective nurseries include the tropical Atlantic Ocean, the Caribbean Sea, and the Gulf of Mexico (collectively known as the Atlantic Basin) mainly from August through October; in the eastern Pacific Basin during July and August; in the western Pacific more frequently in the summer, although they may occur during any month of the year; and the north Indian Ocean. The western Pacific, with its expanse of very warm water, in places exceeding 86°F, is the most fertile for full-blown hurricanes.

Annual fluctuations in the numbers of hurricanes are quite normal, and are tied to seemingly everything: the solar cycle, high altitude winds, temperatures over North Africa, the periodic El Niño current, ice flow near Greenland, North Atlantic salinity, and numerous other factors.

Hurricanes. Tropical atmospheric waves that become tropical depressions that deepen into tropical storms that intensify into hurricanes generally track westward in a long parabolic path across the tropical Atlantic. As they near the West Indies, they tend to recurve northward and back across the Atlantic, influenced by the strength and position of a semipermanent high pressure area normally in residence over the ocean between 30° and 35° north latitude during August and September.

If this so-called Bermuda High is weak, it allows a hurricane to recurve over the Atlantic and away from the land masses. If it is strong and a little north of its usual position, the recurvature may not begin until the hurricane is close to the U.S. coastline. If the Bermuda High is especially strong, a hurricane may not recurve at all, but steer into the Gulf of Mexico or even plow through Central America, to emerge as a differently named storm in the Pacific, as Atlantic Hurricane Cesar did in July 1996 to become Northeast Pacific Hurricane Douglas.

Tropical cyclones have no weather fronts, and whip their highest winds at their lowest altitudes. From the hurricane's nearly calm center, the horizontal wind increases to a maximum, which may exceed 200 mph in severe cases, at a radius between 5 and 60 miles from the center. Beyond that, wind decreases toward the perimeter of the storm's influence, which may lie up to 700 miles distant.

Vertical circulations are strongest in the inflow from the lowest half mile or so, moving at an upward and outward angle, just inside the ring of maximum horizontal winds. This air ascends at an average speed of about 60 feet per minute—but may reach as much as 1,900 feet per minute (22 mph) in some thermals of the cumulonimbus—and exits the thermal in the upper troposphere at about 9 miles, forming a dense cirrostratus cloud shield over the center of the storm.

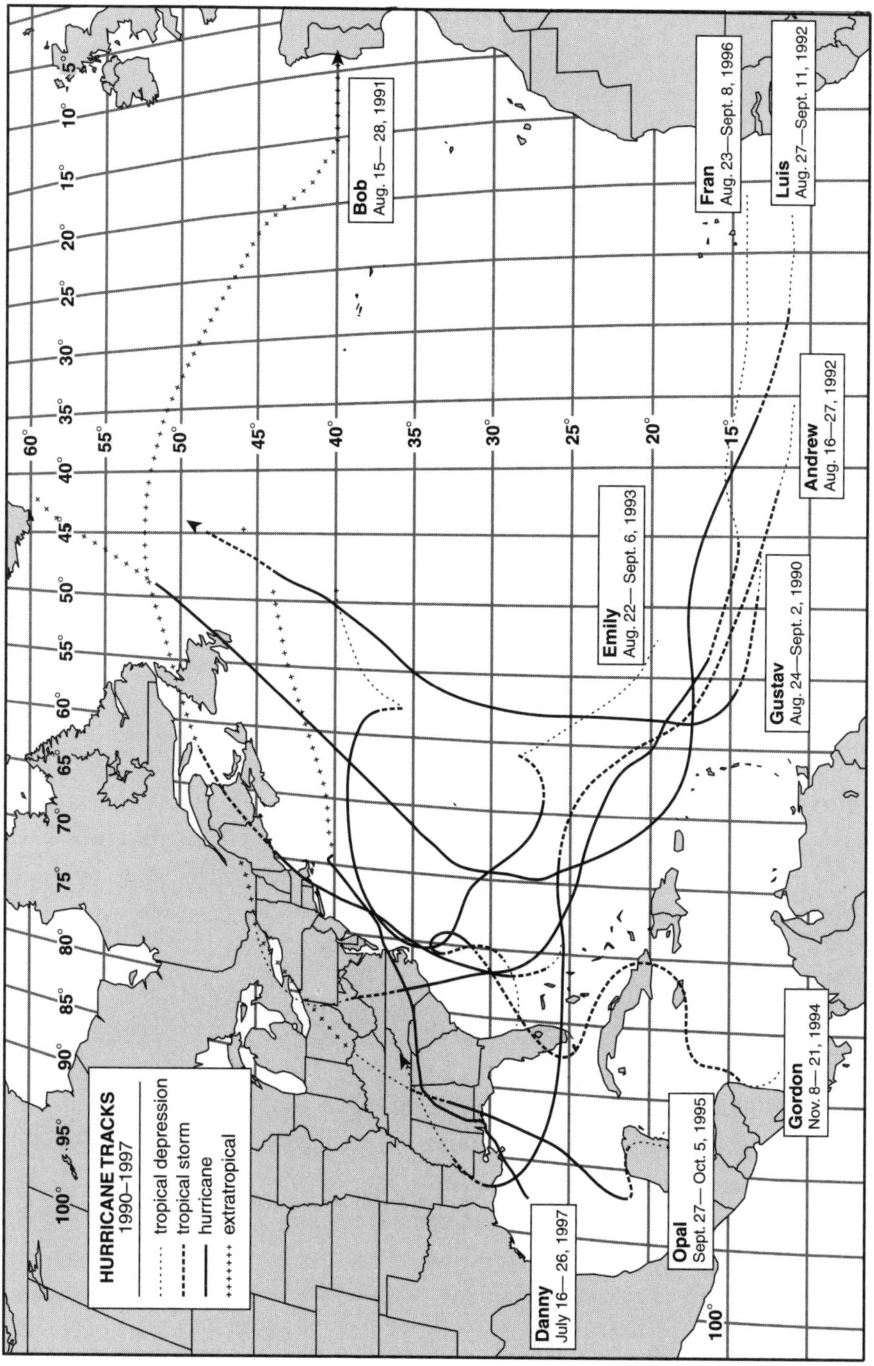

Selected Atlantic Hurricane Tracks

HURRICANE TRACKS
1990–1997

.... tropical depression
– – – – – tropical storm
————— hurricane
+++++++ extratropical

Bob
Aug. 15— 28, 1991

Fran
Aug. 23—Sept. 8, 1996

Luis
Aug. 27—Sept. 11, 1992

Andrew
Aug. 16–27, 1992

Emily
Aug. 22— Sept. 6, 1993

Gustav
Aug. 24—Sept. 2, 1990

Gordon
Nov. 8— 21, 1994

Opal
Sept. 27— Oct. 5, 1995

Danny
July 16— 26, 1997

The hurricane intensifies slowly and steadily as individual plumes join together and build a continuous ring of updrafts, transporting released latent heat upward and maintaining a strong pressure gradient.

At the ocean surface beneath the width of the tropical cyclone, the air temperature is fairly uniform. As the tropical storm matures into a hurricane, the cirrostratus cloud shield disappears, revealing a cloud-free center, or *eye*, in which the temperature increases with height. The air at the top of this warm core circulation may be as much as 18°F warmer than that of undisturbed air at the same altitude. The eye itself can be quite dry, with a relative humidity of

Hurricane Structure (Vertical Cross Section). The hurricane is a giant machine that converts the warmth of the tropical water and air into wind and wave energy through the release of latent heat. Moist convection in a potentially unstable layer, with moist layers in the mid-troposphere, builds clusters of tropical squall lines that begin to rotate with a touch from the Coriolis force. Winds spiral counterclockwise in low-level convergence as they rise through the hurricane. Air flowing out the top of the storm begins curving clockwise in the upper-level anticyclonic divergence.

Hurricane Structure (Horizontal Cross Section). Bands of thunderstorms 3 to 30 miles wide, and 50 to 350 miles long spiral into a clear warm center. The lowest pressure is maintained at the clear eye, the strongest winds in a radius 5 to 60 miles from the center. Precipitation from a hurricane averages 6 to 12 inches as it passes a land location, but can greatly exceed that.

about 50 percent. Most eyes are 18 to 37 miles in diameter, although extremes of 5 to 125 miles have been recorded.

A thick ring of very tall cumulonimbus surrounds the eye, forming the outward-sloping *eyewall*. This angle may be as much as 45 degrees, although it is considerably steeper when the storm is intensifying, or in a small-eyed storm.

Surface relative humidity increases from its tropical norm of 80 percent to near 100 percent at the inner edge of the eyewall, where the bases of the cumulonimbus clouds drop from their average heights of 1,600 feet to nearly touching the ocean water. Vertically, relative humidity remains at saturation or near-saturation levels throughout the eyewall. A dense cirrus and altostratus overcast may extend outward several hundred miles from the center.

Precipitation in the mature hurricane is usually organized into spiral bands about the eyewall. Composed of cumulonimbus clouds spiraling toward the eye, these bands are like ordinary tropical squall lines, but are topped with ice anvils spreading 50 to 75 miles. Low-level convergence and high-level divergence is strongest along these bands, which sets up a direct circulation that leads to increased winds. Warm moist air converges at the surface, rises through the convective band, diverges at the top, then descends on both sides of the band.

SAFFIR-SIMPSON HURRICANE-DAMAGE SCALE

Developed in the early 1970s by Herbert Saffir, a consulting engineer, and Robert Simpson, director of the National Hurricane Center, this widely accepted scale correlates hurricane winds with potential damage.

Category	No.	Damage	Pressure Mb	Wind mph	Storm surge feet	Example at landfall
Depression				<39		
Tropical Storm				39–73		
Hurricane	1	minimal	>980	74–95	3–5	Jerry, 1989
Hurricane	2	moderate	979–965	96–110	6–8	Marilyn, 199
Hurricane	3	extensive	964–945	111–130	9–12	Fran, 1996
Hurricane	4	extreme	944–920	131–155	13–18	Andrew, 199
Hurricane	5	catastrophic	<920	>155	>18	Camille, 196

Closer to the hurricane's center, where the width of clear air between rain bands is much narrower than it is at a greater radius, the subsidence is concentrated into a smaller area, and warms quicker as it descends. Warmer air, being lighter than cooler air, decreases the pressure at a faster rate closer to the center than farther away from it. This difference enhances the pressure gradient across the bands, thus increasing the cyclonic winds around the center.

FACT: Rain gauges in a 1909 hurricane on Jamaica collected over 8 feet in four days! Hurricane Camille dropped 27 inches in a few hours as it soaked Appalachian Virginia in 1969.

On rare occasions, a strong and still-intensifying hurricane may develop a *mesovortex*, of rising, swirling winds about 10 miles in diameter. Sort of like a mini-hurricane within a hurricane, these vortices are about ten times smaller than the diameter of the ring of maximum winds of the hurricane, and about ten times larger than the mile-wide diameter of the individual thunderstorms in the convective bands.

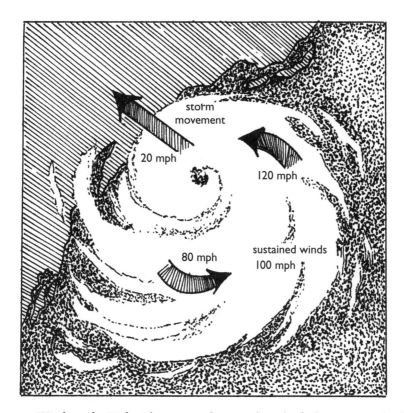

Labels in image: storm movement, 20 mph, 120 mph, 80 mph, sustained winds 100 mph

Stronger Winds to the Right. *The strongest horizontal winds of a hurricane tend to be found on its "right" side (with respect to its direction of travel.) Because the motion of the storm affects the net speed of the air at any point, the forward momentum is added to the right side and subtracted from the left. For example, a stationary hurricane may have peak winds of 100 mph in all quadrants. If this same hurricane moves in any direction at 20 mph, the net wind speed is 120 mph on the right, but 80 mph on the left. Forecasters take this asymmetry into effect and report that such a hurricane's highest winds are 120 mph.*

Should the large cumulonimbus towers of supercell thunderstorms develop near the center of the storm, warm air is pumped directly to the top of the developing core much faster than through the common eyewall route. First identified in Hurricane Hugo in 1989, a mesovortex within the inner eyewall exhibits traits of both small eyewalls and tornadic supercells. Its development results in a sudden, dramatic drop in the sea level pressure, which in turn triggers an eyelike structure of rapid updrafts in remarkably little time and distance.

NAMIN' NAMES

The term hurricane, is derived from *Huracán,* the Caribbean god of evil. The practice of giving names to hurricanes makes sense from the very practical point of having to keep track of them as they develop, grow, and move erratically over hundreds or thousands of miles, and to distinguish them from many others over the years.

Atlantic Basin Tropical Cyclone Name Rotation

2001	2002	2003	2004	2005	2006
Allison	Arthur	Ana	Alex	Arlene	Alberto
Barry	Bertha	Bill	Bonnie	Bret	Beryl
Chantal	Cristóbal	Claudette	Charley	Cindy	Chris
Dean	Dolly	Danny	Danielle	Dennis	Debby
Erin	Edouard	Erika	Earl	Emily	Ernesto
Felix	Fay	Fabian	Frances	Floyd	Florence
Gabrielle	Gustav	Grace	Georges	Gert	Gordon
Humberto	Hanna	Henri	Hermine	Harvey	Helene
Iris	Isidore	Isabel	Ivan	Irene	Isaac
Jerry	Josephine	Juan	Jeanne	Jose	Joyce
Karen	Kyle	Kate	Karl	Katrina	Keith
Lorenzo	Lili	Larry	Lisa	Lenny	Leslie
Michelle	Marco	Mindy	Mitch	Maria	Michael
Noel	Nana	Nicholas	Nicole	Nate	Nadine
Olga	Omar	Odette	Otto	Ophelia	Oscar
Pablo	Paloma	Peter	Paula	Philippe	Patty
Rebekah	Rene	Rose	Richard	Rita	Rafael
Sebastien	Sally	Sam	Shary	Stan	Sandy
Tanya	Teddy	Teresa	Tomas	Tammy	Tony
Van	Vicky	Victor	Virginia	Vince	Valerie
Wendy	Wilfred	Wanda	Walter	Wilma	William

The first person to practice this naming was Australian meteorologist Clement Wragge, who used biblical names (and occasionally the name of a personally despised politico) in the late 1800s. The boys in the Army Meteorological Service during World War II named them for their wives and girlfriends back home. In 1953 the U.S. Weather Bureau began using female names in alphabetical order to christen each year's storms.

Starting in 1978, the U.S. National Weather Service and the World Meteorological Organization changed policies to alternate female names with male names. Separate lists of names were developed for each hurricane basin, and most lists are recycled every six years. Thus the names for the year 2006 will repeat those of the year 2000, and so on. Names beginning with Q, U, X, Y, and Z are not used, and the names of particularly severe hurricanes are retired from the active reserves.

Retired Hurricane Names

Name	Year	Name	Year	Name	Year
Agnes	1972	David	1979	Hilda	1964
Alicia	1983	Diana	1990	Hortense	1996
Allen	1980	Diane	1955	Hugo	1989
Andrew	1992	Donna	1960		
Anita	1977	Dora	1964	Inez	1966
Audrey	1957			Ione	1955
		Edna	1968		
Betsy	1965	Elena	1985	Janet	1955
Beulah	1967	Eloise	1975	Joan	1988
Bob	1991				
		Fifi	1974	Klaus	1990
Camille	1969	Flora	1963		
Carla	1961	Fran	1996	Luis	1995
Carmen	1974	Frederic	1979		
Carol	1965			Marilyn	1995
Celia	1970	Gilbert	1988	Mitch	1998
Cesar	1996	Gloria	1985		
Cleo	1964	Gracie	1959	Opal	1995
Connie	1955	Georges	1998		
				Roxanne	1995
		Hattie	1961		
		Hazel	1954		

The formation of such mesovortexes has been determined to be the cause of the explosive deepening observed in many of the stronger hurricanes. Upon analysis of both the structure and resultant damage of Hurricane Andrew in 1992, the greatest destruction was discovered in the relatively narrow swaths of mesovortex passages.

Most hurricanes strengthen very gradually, but the most intense storms develop a mesovortex and strengthen very rapidly. Hurricane Andrew grew from a category 1 to a category 4 in just thirty-six hours in 1992; it was still intensifying when it met land. Hurricane Camille in 1969, one of only two category 5 storms ever to hit the U.S. mainland, exploded from a category 1 to a 5 in just two days.

While there can be no significant vertical wind shear in the mature hurricane (since it would tear it apart before it could intensify that far), such a difference in the wind profile does develop as the hurricane makes landfall. The sudden friction with the topography of the coast rapidly decays the surface winds much faster than the freely flowing winds aloft, generating just the kind of strong vertical wind shear necessary for spinning off tornadoes. Yet for such destructive wind potential, most storm damage results from all the water traveling with the storm.

Storm Surge. Hurricanes over the ocean, as one would expect, churn a lot of water, and commonly generate dangerous waves upwards of 50 feet in deep water. Hurricane Luis in 1995 worried the *Queen Elizabeth 2* with incredible 98-foot waves!

In the shallower water near land, a different set of worries arises. Despite the lashing from terrible winds and torrential rain, which are considerable, the greatest damages from a hurricane landfall result from its powerful *storm surge*, especially when a storm makes landfall perpendicular to the coastline. The storm surge is a combined-forces effect of lower pressure allowing a

---

NATIONAL WEATHER SERVICE
STORM SURGE SAFETY RULES

1. Know the elevation of your property above mean sea level.
2. Know the evacuation routes for your area.
3. Know the storm surge history for your locale.
4. Do not go sightseeing along the coast when a tropical cyclone threatens.
5. Evacuate when you are told to evacuate.

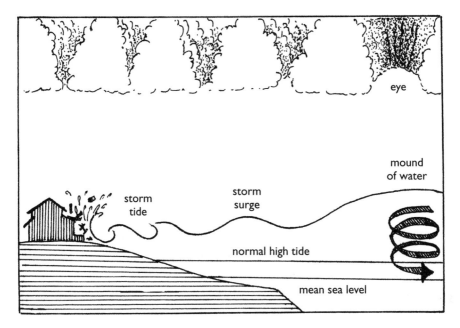

Storm Surge. *The hurricane's spiraling winds push water toward the eye, where it sinks and spreads out in the deep ocean. As the storm approaches land, the shallow slope of the sea bottom prevents the water from spreading out. Instead, it piles up as a mound on the surface and is driven ahead of the hurricane to inundate the coastal plain. The local astronomical tide adds its level to the ultimate depth of the storm tide. The lateral scale in this diagram is greatly condensed.*

general rise in the ocean surface, wind pushing and piling water up as it travels, and the geography of the coast.

Out at sea, the winds spiraling toward the center of the hurricane herd the water in toward the eye. But instead of piling ever higher, the extra water sinks and spreads out, as it would in such a container without walls. But as the storm approaches the shallower bottom of the continental shelf, the water finds containment. With limited place to sink and spread out, the waves amplify and mount up like a tsunami, building an immense mound of water 50 to 100 miles wide to spill out of the ocean, flooding the coast and smashing everything on it. Waves pound the beach mercilessly with destructive force. The steady and forceful wind pushes extra water against the shore.

As the eye approaches, sudden wind shifts drive the water back and forth. An offshore wind pushes some of the excess water back toward the ocean. But with the passage of the eye, an onshore wind shoves even more water back onto the land. If the onshore wind hits first, retreating waves carry off their souvenirs of large debris, adding devastation to destruction.

SYMBOLS: TROPICAL CYCLONES

tropical storm

hurricane

The slope of the seafloor near landfall affects the degree of the storm surge. A gently sloping bottom allows water to build up gradually over distance, creating monster waves. A wide shelf, like that off Long Island or the Mississippi River delta, brings friction to the advancing water over many miles that can produce surges greater than 20 feet high. The steep drop to the deeps around Jamaica, however, offers little chance for water to gang up on the little island.

The storm surge equation is not complete until the positive and negative effects of the local tides are factored in. In 1969, Hurricane Camille's storm surge and the local tide produced a storm tide of 25 feet along the Mississippi coast. Should landfall occur at the time of spring tide, when sun and moon work in conjunction to produce a maximum high tide, the force of the surge becomes all the more deadly.

> **FACT:** In ten minutes, a hurricane generates more energy than all the world's nuclear power plants combined. In one day, a hurricane's winds can produce enough energy to supply the entire United States with electricity for six months.

Case History: Hurricane Opal, 1995.

11 September: A tropical atmospheric wave emerges from the west coast of Africa and begins moving westward.

23 September: The tropical atmospheric wave arrives in the western Caribbean Sea and merges with a low pressure area centered near 15°N, 80°W, about 175 nautical miles due east of the Honduras-Nicaragua coastal border.

25 September: The combined system drifts west-northwestward toward the Yucatán Peninsula, but with no significant further development.

OF TIME AND SPACE

From its embryonic stage as an easterly surface air wave, Hurricane Opal, 1995, moved through six time zones, portions of which were observing Daylight Savings Time. To avoid a great deal of confusion, storm events are usually noted in *Universal Time* (UT), which is the mean solar time at the prime meridian (0° longitude) that runs through Greenwich, England. Universal Time is also known as *Greenwich Mean Time* (GMT) or *Zulu Time* (Z).

To convert Universal Time to local time in the principal time zones of the United States, simply subtract the appropriate number of hours. Atlantic Standard Time is 4 hours earlier than Universal Time. Eastern Standard Time (EST) is 5 hours earlier; CST, 6 hours; MST, 7 hours; and PST, 8 hours. During Daylight Savings, subtract one hour less in each time zone.

Over water, distances are measured in *nautical miles,* which are slightly longer than statute miles. The nautical mile is based on the length of arc along the angles of latitude and longitude on the earth's surface.

> 1 nautical mile = 1 minute of arc
> 60 nautical miles = 60 minutes = 1 degree latitude

Since the actual distance varies with latitude, it is set by international agreement to mean 1,852 meters or 1.15 statute miles.
Winds are generally expressed as *knots* (kts).

> 1 knot = 1 nautical mile per hour = 1.15 miles per hour

27 September: The disturbance becomes a tropical depression (1004 mb; 29 mph) about 70 nautical miles south-southeast of Cozumel, Mexico, at noon local time.

30 September: After slowly moving over the Yucatán Peninsula the past three days, the depression deepens to tropical storm status near the north-central coast and is named Opal at 6 A.M. local time. (1001 mb; 40 mph).

1 October: The storm gradually strengthens and moves westward into the Bay of Campeche; minimum central pressure continues to drop.

2 October: Opal reaches category 1 hurricane status at 6 A.M. local time (973 mb; 74 mph) while centered about 150 nautical miles west of Merida,

Mexico, and about 500 miles south of the Mississippi River delta. A banded eye develops while an upper-level trough moves into the central United States, steering Opal slowly toward the north.

3 October: Opal turns toward the north-northeast, rapidly intensifies and accelerates over water with surface temperatures of 82–84°F. Cumulonimbus towers begin building into the stratosphere, forming a very high and cold cloud shield. A large, well-established upper-level anticyclone over the Gulf of Mexico contributes to the storm's explosive deepening. Central pressure falls 42 mb within 12 hours, and a total of 53 mb in just 24 hours, reaching category 2 status at 1 P.M. local time (965 mb; 98 mph) and category 3 at 7 P.M. local time (953 mb; 115 mph). Intensity of convection increases dramatically as dryer air is advected over the top of an increasingly moist layer in the midlevel of the storm. The eyewall contracts from a diameter of 25.4 miles to 17.4 miles.

4 October: As the top of the cloud deck cools radiationally overnight in the unusually cold tropopause (-117°F), an intense mesovortex with a 9.3-mile diameter forms within the eyewall. The sea level pressure plunges 17 mb and the eye temperature surges to 79°F at the 700-mb height. Lightning clusters about the eye for about a half-hour prior to 4:45 A.M. local time, when Opal reaches category 4 with minimum central pressure of 916 mb, maximum sustained surface winds estimated at 144 mph, with gusts up to 185 mph, and a 10-nautical-mile-wide eye. The hurricane is centered about 250 nautical miles south-southwest of Pensacola, Florida.

Intensity peaks, then diminishes as the eyewall contracts, dissipates, and is replaced by an outer eyewall. The dry air intrusion, which helped to create the convective instability and thunderstorm formation, eventually introduces too much dry air to the core region. A vertical wind shear tilts the eyewall environment toward the northeast. Reduced sea surface temperatures, and the increased upper-level westerly winds also contribute to the storm's weakening.

Opal makes landfall as a category 3 hurricane at 6 P.M. local time at Pensacola Beach, Florida, without a clear-cut eye, moving north-northeast at 23 mph. Minimum central pressure is now at 942 mb, and maximum sustained surface winds, estimated at 115 mph, are confined to a narrow swath at the coast near the extreme eastern tip of Choctawhatchee Bay, midway between Destin and Panama City.

More than 100,000 people flee inland, gridlocking U.S. Route 29 into Alabama and other highways. Those who wait too long are trapped in their homes as the storm roars ashore with 144 mph wind gusts. The 120-mile stretch from Pensacola to Panama City is worst hit as howling winds peel off

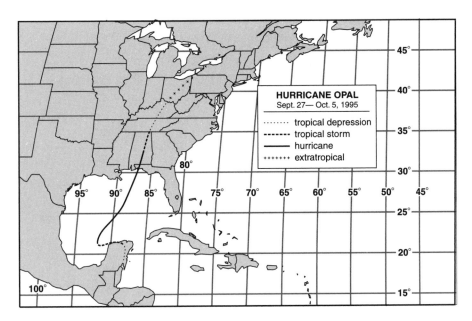

HURRICANE OPAL
Sept. 27— Oct. 5, 1995

········ tropical depression
------- tropical storm
——— hurricane
++++++ extratropical

Hurricane Opal Track

rooftops and 15-foot storm surges flatten shore houses and toss and batter boats into splinters.

Navarre Beach, Florida, 20 miles east of Pensacola, is reduced to rubble: A 15-foot storm surge and 30-foot waves destroy 75 percent of the town's homes; some completely vanish; 25-foot dunes are erased. Large yachts litter Main Street in Fort Walton Beach; a protective barrier of reinforced concrete is pounded into chunks near a Gulf Breeze marina; fifteen large boats are stacked like toys; other ships sink into the harbor amid twisted wreckage. One person is killed by a tornado in Crestview, Florida, the dirty work of one of at least seven spawned by the hurricane. Downpours dump 5 to 10 inches of rain over portions of Florida's panhandle and southern Alabama during the few hours of the hurricane's passage. By 9 P.M. local time, Opal reaches 70 miles south of Montgomery, Alabama, traveling northward at 22 mph with sustained winds of 100 mph.

5 October: Strong winds spread 300 miles inland, knocking out power to nearly 2 million people in Florida, Alabama, Georgia, South Carolina, and North Carolina. More than 7,000 trees at a golf course in Opelika, Alabama, are shoved to the ground. By 1 A.M. local time, center pressure rises to 974 mb and winds reduce to 57 mph as Opal is downgraded to a tropical storm about 30 miles southeast of Birmingham. By midday the storm is about 30 miles northwest of Chattanooga, Tennessee, and again downgraded to tropical

WARNING, WARNING!

High Wind Warning: 1-minute average surface winds of 40 mph or greater lasting 1 hour or longer, or gusts to 58 mph or greater regardless of duration, expected or observed over land.

Gale Warning: 1-minute average surface winds of 35 to 47 knots (40 to 54 mph) lasting 1 hour or longer, either predicted or occurring over water.

Hurricane Warning: Sustained winds 74 mph or greater associated with a hurricane are expected in a specified coastal area in 24 hours or less.

When a Hurricane Watch is issued:

Check often and listen to local officials and bulletins on TV, radio, and NOAA weather radio.

Fuel car; tie down mobile home; tape, board, or shutter windows; wedge sliding glass door tracks; secure loose outdoor furnishings or other materials.

Moor small craft or move to safe shelter.

Check supplies of medicines, canned foods, batteries; stock up.

When a Hurricane Warning is issued:

Check often and listen to local officials and bulletins on TV, radio, and NOAA weather radio.

Stay home if the structure is sturdy and on high ground; board up garage and porch doors; use phone for emergencies only; bring in pets; move valuables to upper floors; fill containers and bathtub with several days' drinking water; turn refrigerator to maximum cold and avoid opening; stay indoors on downwind side away from windows.

Abandon low-lying areas and mobile homes; shut off water, gas, and electricity; leave water and food for pets (shelters do not accept them); take small valuables and papers but travel light; lock up house; leave early, in daylight if possible; drive carefully to nearest designated shelter using recommended evacuation routes.

depression status (982 mb; 34 mph). Highlands, North Carolina, receives 8.95 inches from the storm, and Robinson Creek, North Carolina, records 9.89 inches. By evening, Opal reaches northern Kentucky and is reclassified as an extratropical storm, with central pressure of 986 mb, as winds kick back up to 46 mph.

6 October: Rivers draining into the Gulf of Mexico swell with the excessive runoff. The Blackwater River northeast of Pensacola crests nearly 15 feet above flood stage and inundates sixty homes. From Maryland northward 1 to 3 inches of rain falls throughout the northeastern United States. Storm remnants continue to track northward and pass over Lake Erie, creating a standing wave, a type of storm surge on the lake. The nearly 10,000-square-mile lake first sloshes northward, dropping more than 3 feet along the New York shore, then sloshes back, rising 7 feet above normal. By evening, the system's minimum pressure rises to 1002 mb, with 34 mph winds, and is centered about 17 miles north of Kingston, Ontario.

October 7: Remnant clouds dissipate and winds continue to diminish as the once-fearsome tropical creation drifts northeast over Nova Scotia.

From its tropical wave formation birth to its extratropical storm death, Opal traveled about 7,000 miles in twenty-seven days. The storm killed 59 people: thirty-one in Guatemala flooding during the developing stages, nineteen in Mexico flooding, one from a Florida tornado, two from a tree falling on a mobile home in Alabama, five from falling trees in Georgia, and one from a tree falling on a mobile home in North Carolina.

Insured property damage in the United States totaled $2.1 billion. Additional flood claims, uninsured property damage, and cleanup costs brought the total estimated property damage closer to $3 billion.

Opal is ranked as the fourth most costly and sixteenth most intense hurricane in the United States during the twentieth century.

MIDLATITUDE CYCLONES

These storms are low pressure centers on the move throughout the midlatitudes, ranging from a few hundred miles to a few thousand miles in diameter. These disturbances are the primary distribution systems outside of the tropics for transporting warm air northward and cold air southward—vitally important to the global heat budget and to those of us who live outside of the tropics.

The frontal zones characteristic of the midlatitude cyclone are both a consequence and a result of cyclogenesis. Because we have examined the processes of beginning cyclones, the structures of the various weather fronts,

HYBRID 'CLONES

Subtropical cyclones are hybrid storms that display characteristics of both tropical and extratropical varieties. Like extratropical storms, most subtropical cyclones form from upper-level cold-core lows, and at any time of the year. Like tropical cyclones, they exhibit a ring of maximum wind and rain intensities at a radius from their centers. Once established, they are noted for their persistence, due to closed cyclonic circulations in their upper levels. In Hawaii and some other regions, subtropical storms deliver a large portion of the winter rainfall, and are integral parts of the local hydrologic cycle.

and typical cyclonic weather patterns in chapter 2, we will concentrate here on the winter variation of the cyclone, responsible for most of the wintertime precipitation in the midlatitudes.

> FACT: The energy of a 1-million-square-kilometer cyclone, averaging 20 mph winds throughout its volume, is equivalent every second to the energy released by a 100-megaton thermonuclear bomb. Several such cyclones are occurring at this moment throughout the world.

Winter Snow Makers. The definition of a snowstorm varies from place to place and can be applied to widely disparate storms, over a wide temperature range, in winds ranging from nearly calm to hurricane-force. Extremely wet, heavy snow to very dry, powdery snow can be their products, with every other variation of precipitation in between. There is no difference in the physical structure of a snowstorm from that of a rainstorm; much of what falls as rain begins as snow in the upper levels. The only difference is the temperature profile in which the snow falls. In a snowstorm, the entire column tends to be at or below freezing, while in a raining or sleeting situation, air above freezing exists somewhere between the ground and the level at which the precipitation forms.

Snowstorms differ from other severe weather events in the extent and duration of their effects. Because of sheer size alone, they can affect millions of people over large territories. Snow cover can last for an entire season, even though the storm may have visited for only a few hours. Once a large area is snow-covered, the overall albedo (reflectivity) of the region changes, reflecting more solar radiation back into space, reinforcing cold air at the surface, and maintaining a trough of lower pressure in the upper atmosphere—all of which is conducive to more snowstorms and greater snow accumulations.

For a snowstorm to produce heavy precipitation, there must be ample moisture in the air; and for that precipitation to be snow, it's got to be cold at the cloud level. But to get those two conditions to mix in the same cloud at the same time is the trick. By nature, moisture and cold belong to mutually exclusive clubs. Air that is cold enough to make snow rarely contains much moisture. For heavy snow to fall, there must be a continual source of moisture feeding into the freezing air.

Two special effects, which are not strictly "storms," can produce heavy snowfall by the moisture-feeding method. The first, more common to the western states, is produced as moist air is forced up the sides of the mountain ranges. If the lifting is strong enough, and the temperature is cold enough, the resulting precipitation falls as snow. Snow birthed on windward mountains in this manner is called *upslope snow*. Single-storm totals of upslope snow can exceed 10 feet in the major mountain ranges of the West Coast, and single-season totals of 1,000 inches (over 83 feet!) have been recorded.

The second effect involves a layer of air moving over open water, where it warms and becomes more moist. Convection in the layer begins, drawing moisture upward into thermals. When sufficient moisture is abducted, and the air is cold enough, snow falls downwind of the open water. Named *lake effect snow* after its regular appearance south and east of the Great Lakes, it also forms as subfreezing air moves over open ocean. Heavy amounts of snow can be produced, but it tends to be very localized. The mountains of West Virginia and Vermont regularly receive large amounts of lake effect snow. Salt Lake valley in northern Utah, and even Cape Cod, curled around the bay as it is, both experience lake effect snow from their proximity to open water in winter.

Cyclone Express. In parts of the country where lake effect and upslope snow do not fall, the main snows arrive special delivery via the frontal systems—both cold and warm—of the winter cyclone.

FACT: The shape of spruce trees, which make up the majority of the northern forests, allows excessive snow to simply slide off without damaging the branches.

A cyclone trucks air and water around the countryside, picking up some here, spilling some there. The fuel that stokes this weather machine is the temperature difference between two air masses. Winter storms are more dramatic than their summertime counterparts because temperature differences between air masses are at their most extreme.

During the short days of January in the southern United States, incoming solar radiation is just half of what is received in the long days of July. And winter's low sun grants the northern tier only half of that. Yet that's only part of the

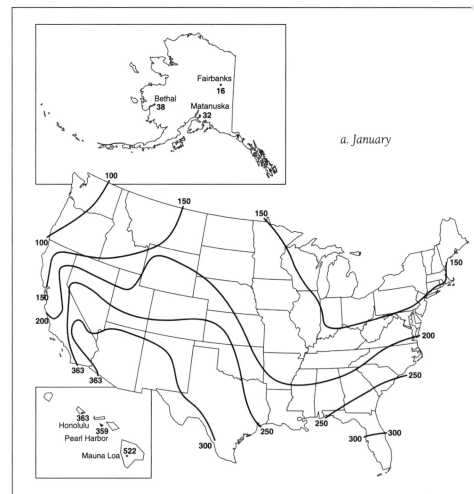

U.S. Mean Monthly Solar Radiation. *While the energy output of the sun does not vary with the season, its angle of incidence on the earth's surface does. The energy*

story. Because land surfaces radiate heat back into space at a constant rate, the northernmost sections of the continent lose heat about twice as fast as the southern parts. Add a snow cover in the north, and the albedo increases dramatically, further reflecting radiation back into space and perpetuating cooler temperatures and greater contrasts between air masses.

Greater north-south temperature differences also increase the vertical wind shear and form jet streams in winter that are about twice as fast as in summer, tending to push weather systems more rapidly eastward.

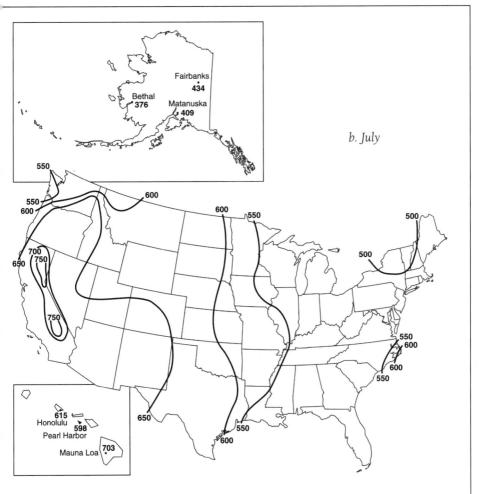

b. July

received in summer is concentrated in a smaller area, and spread over a greater area in winter. Radiation energy is measured in langleys; 1 langley = 1 gram-calorie/cm^2

Given the seasonal settings, conditions are favorable for development of the winter cyclone. As the contrasting air masses meet, the warm air ascends over the cold and its relative density decreases, dropping the pressure at the surface. The vertically moving air is siphoned off at the top of the troposphere by the jet stream, drawing more air up, up, and away, and sending it downstream. Surface air from the surrounding areas—both warm and cold—begins to stream toward the lower pressure, to continue convergence at the surface and divergence aloft, further increasing instability and forming a cycle that feeds itself.

As the forces from the North and South meet in this skirmish, another reckoning force enters the fray and begins to turn things around. The Coriolis effect incites a counterclockwise rotation of the two conflicting air masses, and the winter weather machine has now been cranked and started. Warm moves northward, riding up the rear of Cold. Cold cuts to the south, wedging under Warm's western flank. A storm is born.

The continual fluid motion of the air masses converging, rising, diverging, and sinking means continual changes in the pressure at all levels in the fledgling storm. Such changes produce wind that transports moisture, lifts air and builds the clouds, sinks air and evaporates the clouds, moves the fronts, changes the temperatures. The low pressure intensifies. The cyclone takes on a life and character of its own and begins to move. Riding atop this unbridled creature of the winds, the jet stream points the direction of travel; the cyclone canters more rapidly along its eastward track. Precipitation forms and falls. The winter storm has arrived.

Inside a Snow Storm. What kind of fallout can we expect from a passing winter storm? That all depends.

It depends on the geographic location, the track of the storm, and the storm itself.

In the disharmony of a winter cyclone, where warm air swings up a wedge of retreating cooler air, and where advancing cold air shoves the warm air along in front of it, there's an entire score of vertical temperature profiles, with changes in cadence and dynamics. And there are many variations on the precipitation theme: from wet snow to sleet, to snow grains to freezing rain, to rain and back again, ending with showers of all kinds. It is even possible for a crescendo of thunderous lightning and a cadenza of tumultuous hail in this Snowstorm Symphony, truly a virtuoso performance orchestrated by that humble quartet of Wind, Water, Pressure, and Heat!

The form and amount of precipitation produced by a storm depends on the temperature and moisture content of the warm and cold air masses mashing. As warm, moist air is lifted aloft and cools, precipitable water condenses out into clouds. If the temperature is above freezing, or even slightly below, the vapor condenses into micron-sized cloud droplets. But if it is colder, microscopic ice crystals form instead, and then huddle together in the cold to construct snowflakes. Whether they fall to the ground intact depends on the air beneath them.

> FACT: In strong storms, as warm air is violently forced upward, thunder and lightning may develop, and if the air is sufficiently cold throughout the depth of the storm, the snow produced is known as *thunder snow.*

If the warm air aloft is thick, and so is the cold air beneath it, the snow first melts into rain, then refreezes into ice pellets before it hits the ground. If the layer is thin, it doesn't have enough time to melt before it reenters the subfreezing air, and arrives at the ground as sleet. If the precipitation begins as rain in the warm layer aloft, and the underlying cold air is thin, the rain does not have enough time to solidify while falling, but freezes as glaze as soon as it strikes the cold surface.

As a storm passes by, all the various forms of winter precipitation may debut in one location in succession. As the high clouds make their approach, they may overrun an area where the daytime sun has warmed a shallow layer near the surface. Thus when precipitation starts, it falls from freezing layers above into warmer air at the surface. Wet snow arrives first, but as those freezing flakes float downward, they cool the air around them to the point where the bottom layer returns to subfreezing. Wet snow gives way to regular snow for a few hours.

As the warmer air continues its advance overhead and the cool air retreats, the thickness of the warm layer above increases, and snow changes to snow pellets, to sleet, to freezing rain, and finally to plain rain, as the cold layer at the surface decreases. By the time the warm, moist air penetrates the entire column of air, the bane of the rain stays mainly on the wane: steady rain subsides to showers.

But the storm moves on. Now the front of fresh cold air arrives, shoving ahead the warm air in front. Rain changes back to freezing rain, then sleet, then snow, and finally peters out to snow showers.

For a heavy snowfall, a precise balance in the amount and temperature of the warmer air carried aloft is required. Too much, and rain forms at the highest levels, arriving at the ground as rain, freezing rain, or sleet. Too little, and not enough moisture has been transported upward to produce large amounts of snow.

The section of the cyclone most conducive to these exacting specifications is likely to be north and west of the storm center, in the easterly and northerly flow, with a tail stretching out in front of the warm front. South and east of this region, precipitation is likely to be rain, freezing rain, or sleet. The portion to the north and west of this snowiest zone is likely to see just light snow or snow flurries.

That's the storm. Now for the track of the storm. If you live in the direct path of its center, you might expect the full-length, mixed-precip scenario, lasting six to twelve hours, leaving the disappointing (to some!) net result of frozen ground and a dusting of snow.

A hundred miles to the southeast, and people are saying "What snowstorm?" Initial flurries and snow dwindle to an hour, perhaps, and the mixed precip and rainy period lasts three to six hours, followed by rain showers. The whole thing blows over with a bit of bluster, but not much show of snow.

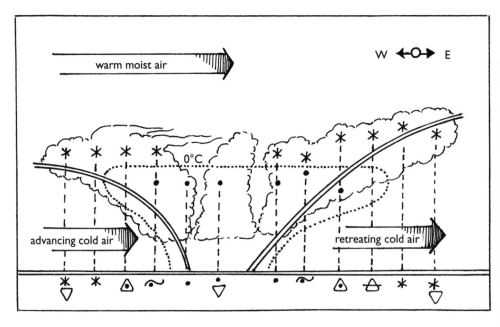

Winter Cyclone (Vertical Cross Section). Precipitation types vary along the frontal systems according to the vertical temperature profiles.

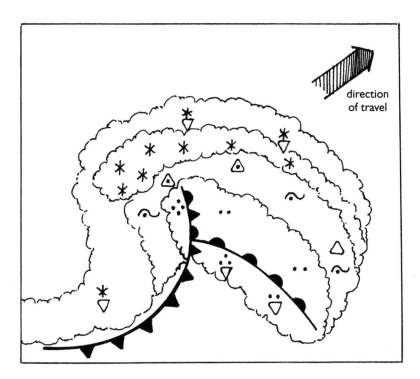

Winter Cyclone (Horizontal Cross Section). *Certain precipitation types are more likely in certain areas of the winter cyclone than others, due to the structure and position of the weather fronts and the overall cyclonic flow.*

However, a hundred miles to the northwest of the storm's track is a whole 'nother ball of ice. An hour of light snow, followed by four or more hours of heavy snow ending with flurries, may leave several inches of dry snow on the ground, with the wind pushing drifts around, and the snow lovers ecstatic.

At its most severe, the storm becomes a *blizzard* if three conditions are met: significant accumulation of .31 inch or greater per hour (or, alternatively, blowing snow reducing visibility to one-quarter mile or less); sustained winds of at least 35 mph; and temperatures of 20°F or less. (This temperature criteria has recently been dropped in some locations.)

A *severe blizzard* rating is warranted when winds mount to a steady 45 mph or greater, visibility drops to near zero, and temperature hovers at just 10°F or lower. The consequences of such a storm produce fatalities. They include wind chill temperatures of −30°F and lower; wind damage; burying snowdrifts; hardship for wildlife; disruption of commerce and traffic; accidents and collapsing structures; interruption of energy distribution, communica-

A BLIZZARD TO REMEMBER

The blizzard of March 12–15, 1993, produced snow at least one foot deep from the Appalachian Mountains east to the Atlantic Ocean, in a continuous swath from Alabama to Nova Scotia. In some locations several feet of snow fell in its passage, marked with killer tornadoes, straight-line wind gusts over 100 mph, record-low sea level pressures, and record cold temperatures. This memorable blizzard resulted in 270 fatalities and property damage estimated at nearly $1.6 billion.

tions, and basic utilities; structure fires from constant heating; and shortages of food, medicine, shelter, and other vital provisions.

In the northeastern United States, many snowstorms are referred to as *nor'easters* because the general wind direction is from the east or northeast. This is true in most snowstorms, wherever they occur, since the structure of a traveling cyclone produces the greatest precipitation in its northeast quadrant. A cyclonically rotating storm near the Atlantic coast, however, has the added available resource of the open ocean to continue a steady influx of moisture into its development.

> FACT: A layer of ice on a pond acts as an insulator for the pond's inhabitants from the extreme weather.

OBSERVATIONS AND ACTIVITIES

Track a Hurricane. Nearly all media sources report on tropical storms and hurricanes as they approach land. These reports can be assembled to document and track their histories.

Materials: NOAA Hurricane Tracking Chart or map of the eastern United States, Mexico, and the Caribbean, showing longitude and latitude; pen, TV, radio, newspaper, Internet access. The tracking charts are available from the National Climatic Data Center (151 Patton Avenue, Room 120, Asheville, NC 28801; (828) 271-4800; www.ncdc.noaa.gov/ol/ncdc.html).

To Know: Tropical storms generally have a life span of a few days to a week or more. If they reach hurricane force, they have enormous potential for

TRAVELING BY CAR
IN WINTER WEATHER

Here are some tips to keep in mind if you plan to take a winter drive.

Check the vehicle's battery, antifreeze and oil, wipers and washer fluid, ignition system, thermostat, lights and hazard flashers, exhaust system, heater and defroster, and brakes. Have four good tires and a spare. Maintain at least a half tank of gas.

Prepare a winter-storm car kit of the following items: sleeping bags; matches and candles; high-calorie, non-perishable food; drinking water; compass; flashlight with extra batteries; newspapers for extra insulation; road maps; shovel; sack of sand; scraper; booster cables; tire chains; fire extinguisher; brightly colored cloth for signal flag; cellular phone or CB radio.

Keep posted to the latest warnings and bulletins on radio or TV.

Dress in clothes for winter conditions: layered clothing, with a warm coat, hat or hood, warm gloves, and boots—even if you plan only to transfer from building to car and car to building. No one ever expects to break down.

Do not travel during a winter storm unless it is a dire emergency; it is better to delay getting home than to never arrive.

Do not leave the car to run for help, in the event you become stuck or trapped unless help is visible within 100 yards. Run the engine sparingly to keep warm. Turn on the dome light for rescuers to find you. Keep the car ventilated by opening a downwind window a crack; make sure the exhaust pipe is not blocked by snow. Exercise, sing, talk; keep active. Huddle for warmth. Someone in the car should always be awake.

destruction and fatalities. Being aware of their existence and trends is being more prepared for their consequences.

To Do: From TV and radio reports and information published in newspapers, magazines, and the Internet, plot the storm's position on the map with its observed dates, times, pressures, and winds. Using the following chart as an example, collect the data to compile a complete history of the storm; attach the plotted position map and news clippings.

TROPICAL STORM TRACKING CHART

Tropical Storm/Hurricane _____ Month _____ Year _____

Information Sources _____

Date	Time	Status	Press.	Winds	Lat.	Long.	Notes

Summary	Date	Time	Location	Notes
Tropical Depression				
Tropical Storm				
Hurricane Cat. 1				
Hurricane Cat. 2				
Hurricane Cat. 3				
Hurricane Cat. 4				
Hurricane Cat. 5				
Extratropical Cyclone				
Landfall(s)				
Minimum Pressure				
Maximum Winds				
Tornadoes				
Storm Surge				
Rainfall Amounts				
Declared Disaster Area				
Sources of Assistance				
Estimated Damages				
Other				

Follow the Snow. Observe and compile data on snowfall for an entire region during the cold season.

Materials: Regional station reports on temperature, snowfall depth, and precipitation from TV, radio, newspaper, Internet, National Weather Service; rain gauge, thermometer, regional map, pencil.

To Know: In many areas, snowfall accounts for a major portion of the region's total annual precipitation, providing important moisture during the growing season and for urban water use. A season's total snowfall may have a profound influence on agriculture and resource use, tourism and recreation, government, industry, and commerce.

To Do: Keep a daily weather record of temperatures and precipitation types and amounts for an entire winter season using regional weather reports. Add your personal observations to others made in your region. Make a graph of the data for each observation station.

Plot total recorded *snowfalls* on a regional map, and analyze the pattern with isolines of equal snowfall.

Prepare another regional map with station observations of *total precipitation,* accounting for the water content of the snow, and analyze with isolines. How do the two maps compare?

Is there any indication of lake effect snow? of upslope snow? Did the snowmelt cause any flooding? Were amounts adequate for expected needs? How did the snowfall affect the people of the region? How did this season compare to those in past years?

Blizzard Field Trip—and Snow Forts. Dress warmly in layers and take a walk in a snowstorm.

Snowdrifts form in predictable patterns as wind deflects around objects at the surface. Scout them out; measure the tallest ones. Compare heights to average snow depth. Scoop a hole into the side of a particularly large one for a shelter: When the wind stings your face with blowing ice, stick your head in it.

Build a snow fort and stock it with snowballs. Engage passers-by in a friendly volley. Explain that you are merely gauging snow moisture content by how well the snow packs.

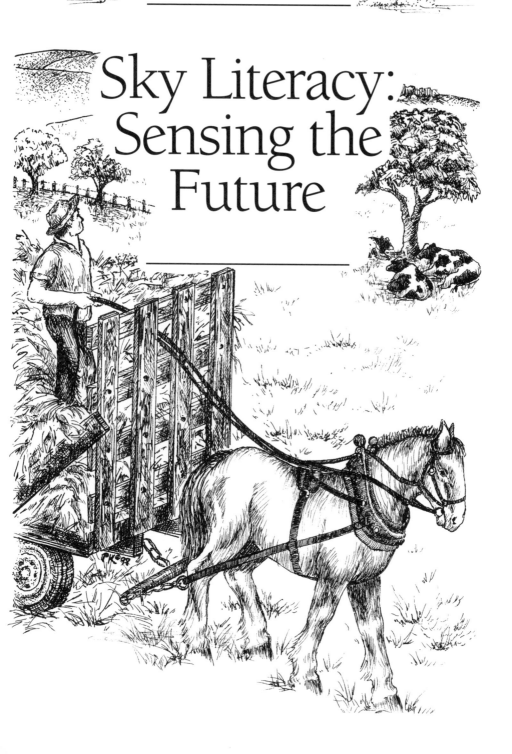

CHAPTER 7

Sky Literacy: Sensing the Future

Anyone with the ability to make some simple observations and keep tuned to what is happening in nature is able to make some surprisingly accurate short-range weather predictions. Being weatherwise is being sensitive to nature. Its condition at any one particular moment is subtly affected by the conditions of the atmosphere at any one moment. Such subtle changes in colors, textures, plant appearances, and animal behavior all have meaning, and, if properly interpreted, reveal additional changes to come.

The weatherlore of observational forecasting is often lumped together with folklore, superstition, and myth and widely regarded as having no scientific value. However, as we early twenty-first-century types need to be reminded, it's only in the past handful of years that we've eschewed the wisdom derived from hundreds of generations' careful observations of the weather, to rely on secondhand observations made by remote-sensing machines and derived numerical forecasts from mathematical models.

Such advanced scientific progress is indispensable, and future development of the atmospheric sciences is promising. There's certainly a place and a need for the technological gadgetry that can better track and model the infinitely complex, real world. But dependence on models and machines removes us a step from real interaction with our environment.

The reality of life is in its experience, and in this chapter we intend to step into the real world. Now that we have a background in the science of basic weather concepts, we can round out that conceptual understanding with firsthand observations to become sky literate: to be able to read the present and interpret the future.

This chapter is split into three parts: a bit of the historical and scientific basis of weatherlore; making personal observations, measurements, and short-range forecasts; and a mention of some of the technological tools the professional meteorologists use.

OBSERVATIONS OF NATURE

Like a lot of old folklore, much of the old-time weatherlore is set to rhymes to aid the memory. But unlike much folklore, most weatherlore is trustworthy because of a basic consistency in nature, with its predictable pattern of cause-and-effect. The same weather patterns that told the ancient Greek when to harvest his grain is the same that speaks to the Iowa farmer today. The trick, then as now, is what these predictable patterns are and what they mean.

On the other hand, since observational forecasting has traveled in the same crowd as folklore and legend through the generations, it's not surprising that some "bad 'uns" have mixed in with the "good 'uns." Some bits of weather "wisdom," especially those that involve a human cause for a desired effect, are blatantly false, not to mention downright silly or dangerous. The ancient Chinese believed that igniting small red firecrackers would bring rain. Medieval Europeans believed that ringing church bells during thunderstorms would stop the lightning. (This belief was struck from accepted practice when one historian noted that 386 church towers were struck by lightning in a 33-year period, with a loss of 103 bellringers!) An American slave myth affirmed that killing a snake causes rain. Everyone today, of course, knows that it takes washing your car.

> FACT: The length of daylight determines the timings of such things as plant blooming, bird migration, fish spawning, and other wildlife reproductive cycles.

It's not always easy to see where some of those absurd beliefs got started, but some do linger. (Don't get me started about the pseudoscience of astrology and how stars can rule your life!) Some other weather/folklore superstitions based on seasonal observations can be just as silly, and speak more about previous conditions than future ones. For example, from the Ozarks: Bad winter is ahead if the muskrat lodges have more logs, or A bad winter is betide, if hair grows thick on a bear's hide. These marvels say more about the past summer being a good one for these critters than about what's ahead for them (and us).

In the northeast United States, folklore prognosticators look to two other furry critters to forecast the length and severity of the winter. Supposedly a long, cold winter is in store if the brown band of the wooly caterpillar (the larval stage of the tiger moth) is narrow. However, not only do individual caterpillars living in the same locale—even mere feet from each other—vary in their coloration, so does the width of their dark bands. And let's not forget the frivolity each February 2 of rousting some poor hibernating groundhog from its den to peer at its shadow—or not. Charles A. Monagan, in his book *The Reluctant Naturalist,* challenges the groundhog's abilities, with a photo of a Cheerios box seeing *its* shadow on February 2, and predicting six more weeks of winter.

Humor aside, these types of predictions, while a part of folklore and our heritage, have become too twisted to be reliable or were never based on fact to begin with. We may simply enjoy them for what they are: fun. For practical daily weather advice, we need to look for those atmospheric and terrestrial signs that do indeed bear out the weather wisdom of the ages.

By taking cues from the sky, trees, flowers, insects, and animals, from aching bunions and bones, and a thousand and one other indicators, the art of weatherlore can lead to accurate short-range forecasts. Observational forecasting requires a certain sensitivity to all of nature in all its forms—its sights, sounds, smells, textures, and even tastes. A simple, practical, and accurate assessment of what the weather is up to can be made by interpreting subtle causes and effects.

This kind of forecasting can be more precise for a certain location than regional forecasts decided by computers inside buildings far away. It is, or should be, serious business to all whose livelihoods depend on the whims of the weather. If misguessed, the farmer can lose his crop; the sailor her life; the hunter his game; the retailer her profit; the salesman his opportunity; the pilot her schedule; the builder his deadline; the athlete her edge; the shipper his cargo.

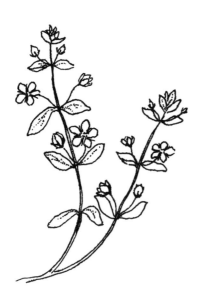

Pimpernel, pimpernel, tell me true
Whether the weather will be fine or no;
No heart can think, no tongue can tell,
The virtues of the pimpernel.

Scarlet Pimpernel. *The scarlet pimpernel has been called the "poor man's weatherglass," for its tiny red flowers that open for sunny days and close for rainy days. A member of the primrose family that grows in sandy soil, its starlike blossoms bloom from June through August.*

Meteorology and weatherlore forecasting share a common heritage. The science of the first measures indicators of pressure, temperature, and humidity with instruments and consults tables of data to produce a forecast. The art of the latter may derive the same forecast, but from more readily available, and more subtle, indicators. An understanding of atmospheric thermodynamics is not required, although it remains the scientific basis for the observations. For example, one old proverb goes like this:

> If the robin sings in the bush
> Then the weather will be coarse;
> If the robin sings on the barn,
> Then the weather will be warm.

OK, so the rhyming is bad, but the observation is good. Because the lower pressure associated with cyclones and storms makes it harder for birds (as well as airplanes) to fly, the robin is likely to stay in its shelter in the immediate hours before a storm hits.

But just as a percentage of the meteorologists' forecasts miss ("bust," as they say), sometimes the weatherlore signs also fail. Nature remains incredibly complex, and almost anything is possible, however improbable. Mariners know anything can happen in unsettled weather, and farmers call off all bets in times of drought. Don't expect absolute accuracy and foolproof sayings.

That said, here's a look at some fairly accurate weatherlore and proverbs, and the science behind them.

Signs of Changes in Temerature. The pretty shrub of the wetland woods with the long evergreen leaves is rhododendron. To the early Americans, it was known as the wild azalea, and they had a saying about it:

> When the wild azalea shuts its doors,
> That's when the winter's tempest roars.

Though the rhododendron's leaves don't fall in autumn, they do drop as the temperature does, as an adaptation to conserve warmth and moisture. It is a true thermometer of the forest, reacting to the cold. At 60°F, the leathery leaves branch out horizontally, broad and dark green. At 40°, they droop. At 30°, they begin to curl, and at 20°, they hang straight down, tightly curled and black.

Crickets and katydids trill and chirp by the means of a stridulating organ on the base of their wings, whose pitch is higher in warmer temperatures. An array of formulas has been developed to correlate the chirping frequency with the temperature, in degrees Fahrenheit. The males' chirps are fairly reliable, but their rate is also influenced by age, success in finding a mate, and other factors. See if you can verify any of the following, or develop your own correlations.

Species	Count the Number of Chirps in	Temperature
Katydid	60 seconds − 40 ÷ 4 + 60 =	
Field cricket	15 seconds + 37 =	
Snowy tree cricket	60 seconds − 40 ÷ 4 + 50 =	
Black field cricket	14 seconds + 40 =	
Others	60 seconds + 100 ÷ 4 =	
	14 seconds + 32 =	

The katydid not only changes its frequency, but its song as well with declining temperatures. At 78°F and above it insists *katy-did-it,* changing its mind at 74°F to *katy-didn't.* By 70°F, it's back to *katy-did,* switching to just *katy* at 65°F, and the monosyllabic *kate* at 58°F, before falling silent below 55°F.

Signs of Changes in Humidity. The moisture content of the air increases as stormy wet weather approaches. In the clearing after a storm's passage, the humidity decreases. This pattern is also associated with advancing and retreating cloud formations.

Here are some sayings to test out:

If clouds be bright,
'Twill clear tonight;
If clouds be dark,
'Twill rain, do you hark?

If wooly fleeces spread the heavenly way,
No rain, be sure, will mar the summer's day.

A rain-topped cloud with flattened base
Carries rain drops on its face.

When hill or mountain has a cap
Within six hours we'll have a drap.

When clouds appear like rocks and towers,
Earth's refreshed by frequent showers.

When halos appear, this rhyme is accurate nearly 80 percent of the time:

> When sun or moon is in its house
> Likely there will be rain without.

Wildlife particularly sensitive to moisture, such as amphibians, tend to be more overtly active in humid conditions, while animals who tend to avoid it, like insects, decrease or alter their normal activities.

> Tree frogs piping during rain indicate that it will continue.

> If toads come out of their holes in great number, it will rain soon.

> When frogs warble, they forecast rain.

> Ants that move their eggs and climb,
> Rain is coming anytime.

> When bees to distance wing their flight,
> Days are warm and skies are bright;
> But when their flight ends near their home,
> Stormy weather is sure to come.

Materials that absorb water will do so in humid conditions, and release it in drier conditions. Notice of such things usually precedes the noticeable changes in the weather.

> Doors and windows are harder to open and shut in damp weather.

> Salt becomes damp before rain.

> Ropes are more difficult to untwist before bad weather.

> Seaweed dry, sunny sky;
> Seaweed wet, rain you'll get.

As the humidity rises, the dew point generally does too, and the more likely it is for dew or condensation to form on cool surfaces, like a concrete garage floor.

> When stones sweat in the afternoon, it indicates rain.

Signs of Changes in Pressure. Falling pressure is a sure sign of an approaching cyclone, and its associated frontal systems, higher winds, and

Barn Swallows. *Swallows are a family of fast-flying, streamlined birds with long, pointed wings and a graceful ease in the air. Their skillful maneuverability and wide mouths enable them to feed almost exclusively on flying insects. With lower pressure and higher humidity, the insects they feed on stay closer to the ground.*

wet weather. Lower pressure, with its less dense air, makes flying more difficult for birds. Sudden changes in pressure affect joints and old injuries, as the greater difference in internal and external pressures cannot be equalized as quickly. Rising pressure is a sign of clearing and the fair weather of anticyclones.

> Swallows fly high: clear blue sky;
> Swallows fly low: rain we shall know.

> Expect fine weather if larks fly high and sing long.

> A coming storm your shooting corns presage,
> And aches will throb, your hollow tooth will rage.

> Martins fly low before and during rain.

Seagull, seagull, sit on the sand,
It's never good weather while you're on the land.

When water rises in wells and springs, rain is approaching.

If kites fly high, fair weather is coming.

Signs of Changes in the Wind. Because of the wind's direct association with the weather—stormy or fair—even the phrase "changes in the wind" has come to mean the inevitability of future events. West and north winds are known for bringing cooler and drier air; south and east winds bring warmer air and rain. Backing winds (shifting counterclockwise) are a sign of an approaching low pressure center. Veering winds (shifting clockwise) foretell of the calmer and fairer, clockwise-rotating winds about a high. Greater wind speeds and higher gusts travel with faster-moving storms and in the steep pressure gradients they create, although the advance warning they give may be very short.

Test these sayings about wind:

Wind in the west,
Weather at its best.

A wind in the south,
Has rain in her mouth.

A southerly wind with showers of rain,
Will bring the wind from the west again.

When the wind is from the east,
Neither good for man nor beast.

Winds that swing against the sun,
And winds that bring the rain are one.
Winds that swing round with the sun,
Keep the rainstorm on the run.

When the wind backs and the pressure falls,
Be on your guard against gales and squalls.

The sharper the blast,
The sooner it's past.

A veering wind will clear the sky,
A backing wind says storms are nigh.

Complementary and Contradictory Signs. Because nature is so diverse, some weather proverbs can be proven factual for more than just one scientific reason. We may even make a case for the truth of some statements that are obviously contradictory. But this can be expected, for everything is inter-related, and contrariness has a part in nature—as well as in the practice of the weatherlore art. Here are a few sprigs of weather wisdom, based on human sensory detection, and their multiple roots.

Higher humidity increases the sense of smell for some people. (You may test yourself by smelling vanilla or some other spice, then wetting the tip of your nose and your upper lip and taking another whiff.) Hence:

When the perfume of flowers is unusually strong, expect rain.

Moreover, areas of lower pressure, being less dense, may allow odors to travel more freely with the currents, as well as release bubbles of gas from the fermenting muck of a swamp, to wit:

When the ditch and pond affect the nose,
Then look out for rain and stormy blows.

Folks with sensitive hearing may detect changes in familiar sounds. Sound vibrations are carried farther in calm, humid, less dense air.

When stringed instruments give forth clear, ringing sounds, there will be fair weather.

On the other hand, a temperature inversion may distort sounds by reflect-ing and refracting acoustic waves back toward the earth (as well as create acoustical mirages!). For example, if an inversion occurs over a river with steep sides, vertically moving sound may be reflected within and constrained to the shallow inversion layer; horizontally moving sound may be reflected from the banks; and sound nearest the river may move at a different speed than that just several meters higher, with the result of an amazing, partially inverted, par-tially repeated, incomprehensible, long-distance call propagating along the river in calm conditions.

On yet another hand, if there is substantial wind, as there often is with approaching storms, vibrating sound waves may be easily carried along as a portion of the moving air for a great distance. Too, an approaching storm's dense cloud cover may reflect a portion of the sound waves back toward the earth, and help make the case for just the opposite atmospheric conditions:

> Sound traveling far and wide
> A stormy day will betide.

Drier air is also clearer air, affording greater visibility of distant objects. With a great amount of water in the air, visibility decreases; as it reaches saturation and mist forms, sight distance is greatly diminished.

> When day is dry, the mountain view
> 'cross valley stream and sky of blue.
> When day is wet, the mountain sleeps
> 'neath foggy mist and sky that weeps.

On the other hand, dry air that has become stagnant often becomes hazy, containing dust and aerosols, while the movement of a coming low pressure area clears the air before the storm. This is especially true with the haze of airborne salts over the ocean's surface. Hence the following proverb, also true, from the old-time mariners:

> The farther the sight,
> the nearer the rain.

Signs of Light through the Atmosphere. The setting sun flashes a full palate of natural colors across the western sky; a rainbow's brilliant arc delights our eyes and commands our attention; "water" shimmers on a hot highway until our approach. Light rays emanate and extend from cloud to horizon; tinted rings encircle the moon; a deep azure sky accents the landscape and beautifies the world. The effects of light traversing the atmosphere produce a fascinating array of optical phenomena—a resplendent bonus for the weather-observant *and* a clue to weather-in-the-making.

Such photometeors (literally, "light-things in the sky") are the luminous results of light interacting with atmospheric conditions. As visible light streams through the atmosphere, encountering air molecules in varying densities, dust of all kinds and sizes, and water in all its phases and forms, it may be bent, split, attenuated, concentrated, deflected, or otherwise diverted along its pathway to our eyes. Four different processes contribute to this, alone or in cahoots: three of them also separate light into its component colors in a neat feat called dispersion. When they get their cumulative act together with the ever-diverse, ever-changing weather, the resultant light show can be astonishing.

Signs of Light through the Atmosphere

Sky Colors. As light enters the top of the atmosphere, it begins to be scattered most at the shorter wavelengths. By the time it reaches our eyes, the short wavelengths have been scattered many times, and the sky appears blue. At sunset, when the light reaching our eyes has passed through a much longer cross section of the atmosphere, most of the shorter wavelengths have been scattered completely away, resulting in the yellows, oranges, and reds of a spectacular sunset. Aerosols of fine dust and ash in the air from pollution or volcanic eruptions, as well as suspended salt particles in the air over oceans, also help to create red sunsets. Water vapor in the air tends to absorb red wavelengths, and in the heavy concentrations before a storm, may cause an ominous greenish pall in the air.

Coronas. When light from the sun or moon passes through the very small water droplets of mist, fog, or a thin cloud, it disperses into its spectrum in a series of concentric rings about the sun or moon called a corona. Coronas are more easily observed in moonlight than sunlight because of the sun's brightness.

Rainbows. The familiar arc of the rainbow is produced as light gets bent inside individual raindrops falling in a sheet, and comes in several varieties. For a rainbow to occur, the sun must be shining in one portion of the sky and rain falling in another portion. For a rainbow to be observed from the earth's surface, the sun must be at the observer's back and the rain in the opposite direction.

When the light dispersed back to our eyes from the raindrops has reflected just once from the back of the drops, we observe the arc of the *primary rainbow,* with red on the top or outside of the arc and violet on the bottom or inside of the rainbow.

A larger, fainter arc of color may form from two reflections inside raindrops. The *secondary rainbow* displays the opposite color scheme of the primary bow, with red on the inside and violet on the outside, having, in effect, turned the color dispersion "inside out" to get to our eyes.

When the two bows are present together, the sky between them is noticeably darker than above and below them because of the absence of light being bent to that region. It is called *Alexander's dark band,* in honor of Alexander of Aphrodisias, who first described it nearly two millennia ago.

In fog or clouds, the same phenomenon forms the wider, less colorful bow of a *fogbow* or a *cloudbow,* also descriptively known as a mistbow or a white rainbow. Occasionally, in bright moonlight, with the presence of raindrops and all the other geometrical requirements, the rainbow's beautiful nighttime version, the *moonbow,* may be observed with its blend of softer, paler colors.

In a sharply defined primary rainbow, several sets of narrow prismatic bands may be observed just inside the violet ring. Called *supernumerary bows,* they are caused as light waves interfere with each other as they exit the raindrop.

Halos. Halos are the generic term for a variety of colored or whitish rings or arcs about the sun or moon, when seen through an ice crystal cloud or in a sky filled with falling ice crystals. The colors of halos result from refraction through the crystals, whose opposing or adjacent faces form essential prisms to disperse the light; whitish effects are the result of reflections from the crystal faces. Randomly oriented small crystals produce the circular halos. Larger crystals tend to settle aerodynamically as they fall into certain specific orientations and form an assortment or arcs about the sun, appearing with or without the circular company.

Many variations of ice crystal optics are possible; some quite rare, but real enough and often intriguingly complex. Some arcs overlap with others, or form within others, or display poorly, making observation and identification difficult. Some have been observed and are fully understood and documented, while the causes of others have yet to be satisfactorily explained. Still others have been only theoretically predicted, and not observed in nature. Suffice it to say that nature's infinite variety, complexity, and beauty remain amazing and awe-inspiring!

Mirages. The mirage is a true thing: a distorted image of real objects caused by light bending through the air. Because the earth's atmosphere is more dense than the vacuum of space, light bends (refracts) to a small degree when it enters it. But at times, when the temperature profile of the air near the surface (and hence its density) develops sharp differences over short distances, light may bend significantly along its path, distorting what can be seen, forming a mirage.

When air temperature decreases rapidly with height, as happens on a sunny day over pavement, the image of a distant object is displaced downward. Blue light coming from the sky may be bent so that it appears as if it is coming from the surface of the earth, looking like water on the ground. Sometimes the upper portions of cars, posts, or trees may be displaced downward, but their lower portions appear as inverted images below them, looking like reflections, although none have occurred.

Scintillation. When observing stars, planets, and other luminous nighttime sky objects outside our atmosphere, rapid variations in their apparent brightness, color, and position may occur. Such *astronomical scintillation* is caused by rather small parcels or layers of air, whose temperatures (and hence densities) differ slightly from those of their immediate surroundings. As these parcels move across our line of sight by the wind, the light from these distant objects refracts through them, producing the irregular fluctuations we see. Scintillation is always more pronounced in objects nearer the horizon than nearer the zenith, due to the greater mixing of the air nearer the surface. On clear, cold nights, stars appear brighter as their light reaches our eyes relatively unmolested by the temperature differences that lead to scintillation.

The Aurora. Making its appearance as beautifully colored curtains of flowing light, the *aurora borealis* (*aurora australis* in the southern hemisphere) would seem to be visible light interacting with the atmosphere—but it's not. It is instead a high-vacuum electrical discharge produced high in the upper atmosphere, above 62 miles. As observed from higher latitudes, the aurora resembles shifting, softly pleated draperies of multiple sheets.

MEASURED OBSERVATIONS

From the patterns of nature, with all their complexity and diversity, emerges a tale of the weather, its influences, and its patterns. To our subjective and qualitative observations of biological and physical behaviors, we now add the objective and quantitative measurements of the air itself. The resultant "bigger picture" becomes a more readable account of the nature of the weather.

By using a few simple instruments to measure and collect weather information, the local current events can be quantified and defined. By recording their readings at least once a day—and at the same time each day—the daily saga of the weather translates itself to practical data, useful in formulating a reliable forecast.

Such daily observations should include looks at both the present and immediate past history of the weather in terms of temperature, humidity, pressure, wind speed and direction, cloud types and sky coverage, precipitation types and amounts, and visibility. An example of a daily weather observation log is included near the end of this chapter.

In meteorological practice, the surface air temperature refers to free air at a height about 4 to 6 feet above ground level, which is representative of where we humans experience it. This temperature can vary quite widely from the air temperature a few inches above the ground. On hot, sunny days and cold frosty nights, the difference can be significant.

To be a fair representative of the temperature at this height, a thermometer should be mounted in a louvered instrument shelter that is painted white. This should be placed so that it is not influenced by artificial conditions, away from any artificial heat sources, such as a wall of a heated building or over pavement that may absorb heat. The door of the shelter should face north to prevent the sun from ever shining on the thermometer bulb. The preferred soil cover under the thermometer is short grass or, where grass doesn't grow, the natural earth surface of the area.

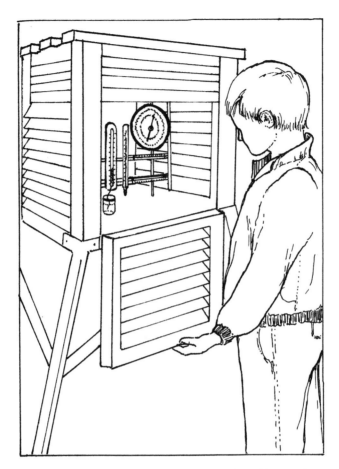

Weather Instrument Shelter. *A louvered instrument shelter allows ambient conditions to exist inside, while sun, wind, and precipitation are excluded. A fully equipped shelter may contain an aneroid barometer, minimum and maximum thermometers, and wet and dry bulb thermometers.*

Air temperatures should be taken at fixed times, together with the extremes of the day. A variety of *maximum/minimum thermometers* are available. The more sensitive ones are separate instruments. The maximum thermometer is one in which mercury is in a constricted glass tube. When the temperature falls after reaching a maximum, the mercury cannot return to the region below the constriction, provided the glass tube is horizontal. It is reset by forcing the mercury below the constriction by swinging it vigorously by hand.

The minimum thermometer, unlike the max, uses alcohol to wet the interior of the glass (mercury does not). A dark-colored glass marker within the alcohol slides along with the alcohol at the end of its column, called the *meniscus.* As the temperature falls, the alcohol in the bulb contracts, drawing the index down toward the bulb by surface tension. When the temperature rises again, the alcohol expands, but there is no force on the marker and it remains stationary at its lowest point. The minimum thermometer is also mounted horizontally, and simply needs to be tilted with the bulb end up to reset the marker to the meniscus.

Less expensive max/min thermometers are constructed with a U-shaped glass tube partially filled with mercury, and a liquid that expands and contracts with temperature. As the temperature increases surrounding the bulb, on the U's top left end, the liquid in the bulb expands, forcing the mercury down on the left side of the U and up on the right side, pushing a marker along at the top of the meniscus. The bottom of this index marks the maximum temperature on the right-hand scale.

When the temperature decreases surrounding the bulb, the liquid contracts, and mercury moves down on the right side and up on the left side, again pushing a marker along at the top of the mercury meniscus of the left side. The bottom of this index marks the minimum temperature, as read from an inverted scale on the left side.

Both markers are reset manually by using a magnet to pull them back to the tops of the mercury in each side of the tube. Horizontally oriented max/min thermometers of this type are reset by simply tilting the unit to allow the markers to slide back against the mercury.

FACT: Some members of the Gentian family of wildflowers open and close their flowers when the temperature changes as little as one-quarter of one degree.

Humidity. The amount of moisture in the air is a critical factor in the weather—in its contributions to clouds and precipitation, in its phase changes and latent heat, in its land-sea-sky interaction, and in its worldwide distribution. It's also the most difficult component to measure.

Humidity measurements are divided into two groups: those that measure the actual quantity of water in the air, and those that compare the actual amount of vapor to the potential amount that could exist if the air parcel were saturated.

The actual measures include *absolute humidity,* which is the absolute mass of vapor in a given volume; *vapor pressure,* which is the partial pressure attributed to the water vapor; and *saturation vapor pressure,* which is the partial pressure of water vapor in saturated air.

Among the many comparative measures, we are most interested in *relative humidity,* which is the actual vapor pressure divided by the saturation vapor pressure. Of all the moisture measurements, the relative humidity has the most practical use to the amateur weather forecaster and is the simplest to measure.

Hygrometers are the instruments used to measure the moisture content of the air. Since there are many ways to express it, there are almost as many types of hygrometers. A simple hygrometer is made with blond human hair, which has the property of elongating with humidity. Its change in length is linked to a mechanism that registers relative humidity.

Another simple hygrometer that measures relative humidity is the *psychrometer,* consisting of a pair of thermometers, one of which has a piece of wetted cotton on its bulb. As water evaporates from the wet wick on the bulb, the air near its surface is cooled as the water absorbs heat from its surroundings to evaporate. The amount of evaporation depends on how much moisture is in the air already. At saturation, no more net evaporation into the air is possible, and the readings are equal for wet and dry bulbs; hence the relative humidity is 100 percent. At lesser humidity, the wet bulb will be at a lower temperature than the dry bulb. A table to compare the difference between the bulbs is consulted to determine the relative humidity (see table near the end of this chapter).

A sling *psychrometer* is operated by twirling the instrument in the air; the Assmann psychrometer uses a fan to achieve the readings.

Other types of hygrometers use materials such as carbon, lithium chloride, or polymer films that undergo or detect chemical, physical, or electrical changes as they absorb moisture. Microwave radiometers use spectral technology to remotely sense water vapor from the surface or from satellites.

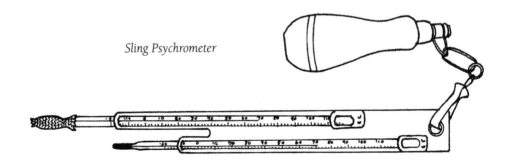

Sling Psychrometer

DISCOVER NATURE IN THE WEATHER

Lasers are used in ground-based sensing, and a new technology infers water vapor concentrations from the atmosphere's index of refraction and the associated variations in the speed of transmitting radio waves.

Pressure. The pressure of the atmosphere is the force generated on a surface area by the total weight of a vertical column of air directly above it, extending to the outer limits of the atmosphere. Near the earth's surface this force is approximately equal to 1,000 millibars (mb), or about 30 inches of mercury.

A barometer to measure atmospheric pressure should be mounted or placed in a solid location that protects against vibrations and remains in uniform temperature and humidity conditions. Along with the present pressure, the tendency of the pressure during the past three hours should also be noted, which indicates more changes to come. Along with the wind direction, the barometric pressure and tendency indicate certain predictable weather patterns. The following table summarizes these patterns and can be consulted to produce a fairly accurate short-range forecast.

Wind. Wind direction is the direction from which the wind is blowing and can be expressed in terms of the points of the compass or as angular degrees measured clockwise from geographical north.

To obtain comparable readings on surface winds among a network of stations, wind direction and wind speed are measured at a standard height of 10 meters (33 feet) above the ground. This is to avoid small-scale eddies and other flow disturbances from local structures, vegetation, and terrain irregularities.

Together, wind direction and speed compose the *wind velocity*. Surface wind velocity is seldom constant and varies almost continuously. Such variations are termed the *gustiness* of the wind. For overall purposes, a 10-minute average of the wind velocity is required and noted.

Speed is measured in knots; for casual observers, knots and miles per hour can be considered approximately equal at lower speeds. One knot—that is, one nautical mile per hour—equals 1.15 miles per hour. The gust term is reserved for a difference from the ten-minute average of at least 10 knots.

Wind vanes point into the wind to show the direction of the wind. They range in complexity from a simple wind sock or flag, to a pointer on a rotating bearing, to recording vanes.

Anemometers measure the wind speed, and range from handheld wind meters, to mounted and rotating cups, rotors, or propellers, to pressure-tube devices that derive wind speeds from the differences in pressure as the wind blows into a tube and as it blows across a tube.

TYPICAL WIND AND PRESSURE PATTERNS

Wind Direction	Barometric Pressure & Tendency			Weather Indications
	in. mercury	mb		
SW to NW	30.10–30.20	1019–1023	steady	Fair with slight temperature changes for 24–48 hours
SW to NW	30.10–30.20	1019–1023	rising rapidly	Fair, followed by precipitation within 48 hours
SW to NW	30.20 & above	1023 & above	steady	Continued fair, with no significant temp. change
SW to NW	30.20 & above	1023 & above	falling slowly	Slowly rising temperature and fair next 48 hours
S to SE	30.10–30.20	1019–1023	falling slowly	Precipitation within 24 hours
S to SE	30.10–30.20	1019–1023	falling rapidly	Increasing wind, precipitation within 12–24 hours
SE to NE	30.10–30.20	1019–1023	falling slowly	Precipitation within 12–18 hours
SE to NE	30.10–30.20	1019–1023	falling rapidly	Increasing wind, precipitation within 12 hours
SE to NE	30.00 & below	1016 & below	falling slowly	Precipitation continues 24–48 hours
SE to NE	30.00 & below	1016 & below	falling rapidly	Precipitation, with high wind, followed by clearing within 36 hours, and in winter, by colder temps.
E to NE	30.10 & above	1019 & above	falling slowly	Summer: light wind, rain not for several days Winter: precipitation within 24 hours
E to NE	30.10 & above	1019 & above	falling rapidly	Summer: rain probably within 12–24 hours Winter: precipitation with increasing winds

TYPICAL WIND AND PRESSURE PATTERNS *(continued)*

Wind Direction	Barometric Pressure & Tendency			Weather Indications
	in. mercury	mb		
S to SW	30.00 & below	1016 & below	rising slowly	Clearing within a few hours, then fair for several days
S to E	29.80 & below	1009 & below	falling rapidly	Severe storm imminent, clearing within 24 hours, followed by colder in winter
E to N	29.80 & below	1009 & below	falling rapidly	Severe gale and heavy precipitation; in winter followed by colder temperatures
toward W	29.80 & below	1009 & below	rising rapidly	Clearing and colder

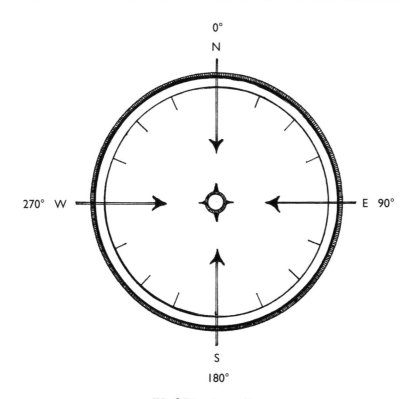

Wind Direction as Degrees

SYMBOLS: WIND DIRECTION AND SPEED

When the wind velocity at a station is noted on a synoptic weather map, a small circle represents the station, and a staff is drawn to the circle at the proper angle to show wind direction. A series of barbs are added to the staff in combinations to indicate wind speed: a short barb for 5 knots, a long barb for 10 knots, and a pennant for 50 knots.

knots	mph	knots	mph
calm	calm	18–22	21–25
1–2	1–2	48–52	55–60
3–7	3–8	58–62	67–71
8–12	9–14	103–107	119–123
13–17	15–20		

In the absence of instruments, an observer may make fairly accurate estimates of wind speed by using the *Beaufort Scale of Wind Force*. Wind direction may be estimated by observing a wind sock, flag, drift of smoke, or movements of leaves or swaying of trees. In many cases, the surface wind direction can be accurately estimated by simply facing into the wind. Stand on open, flat terrain as far as possible from obstructions; be sure to avoid local eddies around buildings and other obstructions. Do not take into account the movement of clouds, however low, because the wind at their levels may be quite different.

FACT: Most birds take off flying into the wind.

BEAUFORT SCALE OF WIND FORCE

A system to estimate wind speed without the use of an anemometer was invented by Admiral Francis Beaufort of the British Navy in 1805. Originally based on the effects of various wind speeds on the amount of canvas a full-rigged frigate of the period could carry, it has since been modernized for both land and sea use.

Force	Speed (mph)	Effects on Land	Beaufort Number	Effects on Sea	Speed (knots)
Calm	<1	Calm; smoke rises vertically	0	Sea like mirror	<1
Light air	1–3	Smoke drift shows wind direction; tree leaves barely move	1	Ripples with appearance of "fish scales"; no foam crests	1–3
Light breeze	4–7	Wind felt on face; leaves rustle; small twigs move	2	Small wavelets; crests of glassy appearance, not breaking	4–6
Gentle breeze	8–12	Leaves, small twigs in constant motion; dry leaves blow up from ground	3	Large wavelets; crests begin to break; scattered whitecaps	7–10
Moderate breeze	13–18	Small branches move; dust and paper rise and blow along	4	Small waves, becoming longer; numerous whitecaps	11–16
Fresh breeze	19–24	Large branches and small trees sway; crested wavelets form on inland water	5	Moderate waves, becoming longer; many whitecaps, some spray	17–21
Strong breeze	25–31	Large branches in continuous motion; whistling heard in wires	6	Larger waves forming; whitecaps everywhere; more spray	22–27

Force	Speed (mph)	Effects on Land	Beaufort Number	Effects on Sea	Speed (knots)
Moderate gale	32–38	Whole trees in motion; resistance felt in walking against wind	7	Sea heaps up; white foam from breaking waves begins to be blown in streaks	28–33
Fresh gale	39–46	Twigs and small branches break off trees; difficult to walk	8	Moderately high waves of greater length; foam is blown in well-marked streaks	34–40
Strong gale	47–54	Slight structural damage; chimney bricks loosened; ground littered with broken limbs	9	High waves; sea begins to roll; dense streaks of foam; spray may reduce visibility	41–47
Whole gale	55–63	Trees uprooted; considerable structural damage; seldom experienced	10	Very high waves with overhanging crests; sea takes white appearance; visibility reduced	48–55
Storm	64–72	Widespread damage; very rarely experienced	11	Exceptionally high waves; sea covered with white foam patches	56–63
Hurricane force	>73	Severe, extensive damage	12	Air filled with foam; sea completely white with driving spray; visibility greatly reduced	>64

Clouds. Changes in wind direction and speed are often linked to changes in cloud types and sky coverage. And because cloud types are closely associated with both the present weather and that to come, it is important to note them. Refer to chapter 4 on the various cloud species and varieties, or consult a cloud chart of photographs. Because wild clouds don't always fit into the neatly domesticated categories, it is helpful to keep a continuous watch on them and note the changes as they develop from one basic type to another. A much more thorough understanding of the weather and its patterns develops this way, than from a once-a-day examination at observation time.

The official measurement unit of cloud amount is one-eighth of the sky, appropriately called the *okta*. The sky coverage should be estimated by supposing that all the clouds present were brought together into one continuous sheet. Divide the sky into four equal quadrants, estimate the amount in each quadrant separately, then add them together. Sometimes it is helpful to estimate the amount of a specific type of cloud. If fog or dust or smoke prohibits a view of the sky, it is said to be obscured. (The sky coverage may also be estimated in tenths of the sky, rather than eights.).

Rain and Snow. Precipitation reaches the ground in many different varieties, and the purpose in measuring the amount that falls is to determine its distribution in both time and space. The total reaching the ground is measured as the depth to which it would cover a horizontal, impervious surface, with no runoff or evaporation. Frozen precipitation is measured as its melted equivalent. Snowfall is measured both as the depth that fresh snow covers an even, flat surface, and as its liquid water equivalent.

A simple *rain gauge* is a straight-sided cylinder, open at the top. Graduated markings etched or molded into the cylinder are used to measure the rainfall amount.

Many rain gauges consist of a funnel on the top of a cylindrical can, which is partly sunk into the ground. The precipitation that falls through the opening is funneled into a smaller cylinder inside the larger one. This narrow inner can is sufficient for most rainfalls, but if it isn't, and overflows, the excess is still contained by the larger cylinder. Measurements are made to the nearest hundredth of an inch.

The size of a gauge's opening is not important, but a dip rod or graduated cylinder used to measure the amount must be consistent with the ratio of the funnel's cross-sectional area to the collection cylinder's. A gauge with a wider aperture than its collection tube allows smaller amounts to be more easily measured—and less chance of a collection error because of wind-driven rain missing the opening or of snow clogging it.

Recording rain gauges are used to provide a continuous record of rainfall duration, intensity, and amount, and also come in several varieties.

Careful consideration must be given to the placement of a rain gauge, to accurately represent the precipitation falling on the surrounding area. It must be away from buildings and trees that would shelter it from slanted precipitation or would create wind eddies that carry precipitation away from or into the gauge. Whenever possible, the gauge should be exposed with its mouth horizontal over level ground, and no closer to an object than the distance equivalent to four times its height. On the other hand, a well-exposed gauge should be sheltered from the full force of the wind. One kind of common baffle consists of a surrounding ring of free-swinging metal leaves to break up the wind flow.

Measuring snowfall depth is a bit tricky. A simple graduated ruler or scale may be inserted into the fresh snow, and its depth measured directly. However, this works best only in the absence of strong winds. Most of the time, a number of vertical measurements must be taken in places considered to be driftless, and the results averaged. Care must be taken not to measure old snow in this method.

A *snowboard*—a square-foot piece of board, painted white—can be used as a base on which to measure fresh snowfall, then cleared after each measurement. The same placement precautions for a snowboard should be considered as those for a rain gauge, since snow accumulation is even more susceptible to the effects of the wind. Several snowboards may be placed in an area with frequent winds and drifting snow.

Water content of snow may be calculated by one of three methods. Immediate readings of ordinary rain gauges or recording instruments may be used, and the collected amounts of snow melted and measured. In another method, a special snow sampler can be used to cut cylindrical samples of snow depth, which can then be weighed or melted. The easiest, but least accurate way is to accept the approximate relationship that 10 inches of fresh snow equals 1 inch of water—a simple 10:1 ratio.

Visibility. Visibility refers to the horizontal transparency of the atmosphere and is a measure of the presence of liquid or solid particles in the air. These may include all the various types of dust and smoke.

The primary measuring instrument is one consisting of a pair of sensors with a frequency response of .4 to .76 microns, an angular response of 90 degrees, an angular resolution of .02 degree, and a time resolution of .1 second. The sensors are connected to an on-line computer that controls their direction and rate of scanning and processes the data. Sensor models come in shades of blue, brown, green, or gray, and billions of these remarkable instruments are in continual daily use around the world.

You guessed it—we're talking about the eyes of human beings. And visibility is defined as the greatest distance at which a black object can be seen with the naked *eye* and recognized with the *brain* against the horizon sky. It is expressed in miles, or fractions of a mile.

Weather Notes. Whenever observations are made and recorded, any other condition of the weather not included in the other measurements should be noted. This may include a statement on the atmospheric conditions, state of the ground, or other phenomena occurring within sight of the station during the observation.

The time of observation is conventionally regarded as a ten-minute period during which the observations are made. Should a shower or intermittent rain occur sometime during this period, it is regarded as current. A thunderstorm may be regarded as currently at the station if thunder is heard, even though it may not be directly overhead. Intensity of precipitation should be noted, as well as, in low temperatures, whether it is freezing or not.

HIGH-TECH OBSERVATIONS

Professional meteorologists combine natural and measured observations of weather at the surface with data collected, derived, and analyzed from many levels of the atmosphere and from all over the world. Observations are made from networks of weather balloons, land stations, ships at sea, weather buoys, and orbiting satellites with high-tech remote sensing equipment. Supercomputers crunch the numbers from the huge supply of raw data into model equations of atmospheric fluid dynamics to produce long-range forecasts. The following briefly describes a few of these valuable tools of the professional forecaster.

Radiosonde. Vertical profiles of wind, temperature, humidity, and pressure, called *atmospheric soundings,* are obtained by weather balloons carrying expendable packages of instruments known as *radiosondes.* Launched twice a day from about 550 stations around the world, at noon and midnight GMT, the balloons rise to a pressure altitude of about 25 mb as the radiosondes transmit measurements back to receivers at the launch stations. The balloons are tracked by optical methods, radio signals, or radar to determine upper-level winds. A new wind-finding technology uses the satellite-based global positioning system to obtain precise worldwide measurements. *Rawinsonde* instrument packages add wind speed to the collected data as they are monitored from the ground by tracking antennae.

Radar. The *Doppler weather surveillance radar* detects particles of water, dust, and ice in the atmosphere and how fast they are moving in a certain direction. It then uses this information to calculate the speed and direction of wind motions and provide early detection and warning of severe weather events. A network of 161 radars spans the entire United States and its island territories from Guam to Puerto Rico.

Radar *wind profilers* measure speed and direction of upper air winds from the ground by beaming radio waves upward at many angles. The waves reflect from slight density gradients in the air back to a sensitive phased-array antenna, which forwards the signals to computers to analyze and compute wind velocities every six minutes at seventy-two different levels up to 10 miles high.

Weather Satellites. Weather satellites have substantially expanded their role in monitoring the weather ever since the first one beamed back photos of earth's clouds in 1960. Today, a number of environment-sensitive satellites at different levels contribute valuable information to the overall picture of the atmospheric condition.

The Polar-orbiting Operational Environmental Satellite (POES) system provides global meteorological coverage, making 14.1 polar orbits a day at a height of 530 miles.

From an altitude of 22,238 miles above the equator, the Geostationary Operational Environmental Satellite (GOES) system keeps pace with earth's rotation to make four observations per hour over the United States, or as many as one per minute over smaller areas of severe weather.

Besides producing the excellent cloud photos seen daily on TV broadcasts, these high high-tech travelers take infrared photos to derive cloud-top temperatures and movements of water vapor, sense temperatures and humidities of land and ocean surfaces and upper air levels, derive wind speeds and directions from cloud movements, and detect changes in radiation.

Supercomputers. Numerical modeling, and the important contributions it makes to long-range forecasts, would not be possible without *supercomputers* capable of digesting millions of bits of data a day. These models encompass a wide range of techniques to solve extremely complex mathematical equations that govern the physics of fluid motion. Data is collected from vast three-dimensional grids around the world and entered into a global telecommunications network. The data is first analyzed to define the state of the atmosphere at the starting time for the forecast, then a forecast is produced by repeatedly solving the equations to produce a new set of variables for each grid point, at

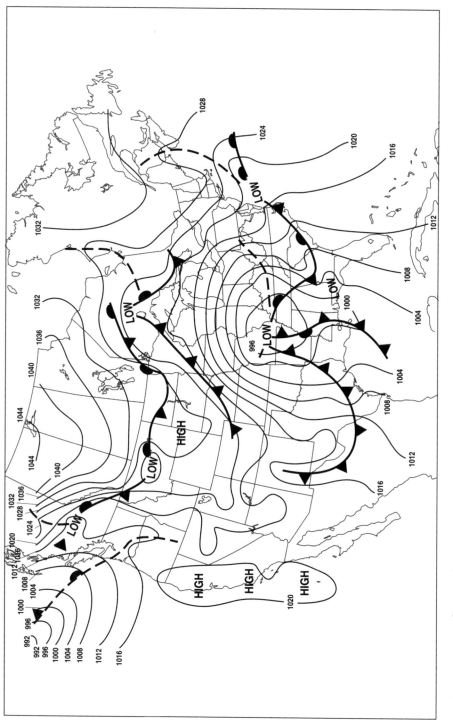

*U.S. **Synoptic Surface Analysis.** 8 March 1998, 7:00 A.M. EST. Compare with the 500 mb height contours of the same date and time on page 45.*

a time a few minutes in the future. The process continues until a forecast for the desired length of time is produced. A ten-day forecast may require the calculation of 1,000 or more individual forecasts, based on the solving of more than a trillion calculations. The sheer complexity and magnitude of an atmosphere in motion, and the affect it has on simply everything, is at once exasperating and exhilarating.

OBSERVATIONS AND ACTIVITIES

Watch the Weather. Create your own instrumented weather station, and make daily observations and forecasts.

Materials: Weather instruments: maximum/minimum thermometer, hygrometer, barometer, wind vane and anemometer, rain gauge, weather log (see the accompanying daily weather observation log).

To Know: Daily weather observations not only track weather systems and patterns, but allow the amateur forecaster to make fairly accurate short-range predictions.

To Do: Set up your own weather station, as described earlier in this chapter in the sections on the various instruments used to measure temperature, humidity, pressure, wind, and rain. Record daily observations on the weather log and make your own forecast for the next day. Chart your forecast accuracy and learn from mistakes and experience. Summarize monthly data, and graph means, extremes, and totals. Compare your station's monthly and yearly data to the regional climate data.

Become a severe-weather spotter for the National Weather Service, or inquire about becoming a Cooperative Weather Station. Contact your local Weather Service office and ask for the Co-op Station Manager. Log on to on-line weather services to observe real-time synoptic surface and upper-air analyses. Compare satellite photos and radar images with surfaces analyses; practice until you know what features to look for.

A Simple Psychrometer. Measure the relative humidity with a home-made psychrometer.

Materials: Two identical thermometers, cotton shoelace, scissors, thread, small jar, water.

To Know: Water in the wick of a wet bulb thermometer absorbs heat from the surrounding air to evaporate, which is measured as a lower wet bulb temperature. The difference between the wet bulb and the dry bulb temperatures is used to determine the relative humidity of the air.

DAILY WEATHER OBSERVATIONS   MONTH _____

	Time	Temperature curr.	max.	min.	RH	Press.	Wind direct	speed	Cloud Type	Sky Cov.	Vis.	Precipitation type	amt.	Notes
1														
2														
3														
4														
5														
6														
7														
8														
9														
10														
11														
12														
13														
14														
15														
16														
17														
18														
19														
20														
21														
22														
23														
24														
25														
26														
27														
28														
29														
30														
31														

SUMMARY	Data	Date	Notes
Mean Temperature			
Max. Temperature			
Min. Temperature			
Max. Pressure			
Min. Pressure			
Max. Wind Gust			
Total Precipitation			

STATION

_____

OBSERVER

_____

Daily Weather Observation Log

PSYCHROMETRIC TABLE FOR RELATIVE HUMIDITY

DRY BULB TEMPERATURE °F

WET BULB TEMPERATURE °F

RELATIVE HUMIDITY

Wet \ Dry	40	42	44	46	48	50	52	54	56	58	60	62	64	66	68	70	72	74	76	78	80	82	84	86	88	90
30	24	14	6																							
32	38	28	18	10	3																					
34	53	41	31	22	14	7	1																			
36	68	55	44	34	25	17	10	2																		
38	84	70	57	46	36	28	20	14	8	3																
40	100	85	71	59	48	39	31	23	17	11	6	2														
42		100	85	72	60	50	41	33	26	20	14	10	5	2												
44			100	86	73	62	52	43	35	29	23	17	12	8	5	1										
46				100	86	74	63	54	45	38	31	25	20	15	11	7	4	1								
48					100	87	75	65	55	47	40	33	27	22	18	14	10	7	4	1						
50						100	87	76	66	57	49	42	35	30	24	20	16	12	9	6	4	2				
52							100	88	77	67	58	52	43	37	32	27	22	18	15	11	9	6	4	2		
54								100	88	78	68	60	52	45	39	33	29	24	20	17	14	11	8	6	4	2
56									100	89	78	69	61	53	47	41	35	30	26	22	19	16	13	10	8	6
58										100	89	79	70	62	55	48	42	37	32	28	24	21	17	15	12	10
60											100	89	80	71	63	56	50	44	38	34	30	26	22	19	16	14
62												100	90	80	72	64	57	51	45	40	35	31	27	24	21	18
64													100	90	81	72	65	58	52	46	41	37	33	29	25	22
66														100	90	81	73	66	59	53	48	43	38	34	30	27
68															100	90	82	74	67	60	54	49	44	39	35	32
70																100	91	82	74	67	61	55	50	45	41	37
72																	100	91	83	75	68	62	56	51	46	42
74																		100	91	83	76	69	63	57	52	47
76																			100	91	83	76	70	63	58	53
78																				100	92	84	77	70	64	59
80																					100	92	84	77	71	65
82																						100	92	84	78	71
84																							100	92	85	78

To Do: Check the readings of the two thermometers to be sure they agree. Mount them side by side. Cut the shoelace to a length of about four inches or so; slip one end on one of the thermometer bulbs, and tie it on with thread. Put the other end of the shoelace into the small jar of water; it will act as a wick to keep the bulb wet. Once the temperature of the wet bulb stabilizes, read both dry bulb and wet bulb thermometers; consult the accompanying relative humidity table to determine the relative humidity.

Catch a Falling Raindrop. Make simple rain gauges; measure raindrop sizes.

Materials: Several straight-sided cans, plastic ruler, shallow tray, flour.

To Know: Rainfall distribution patterns and amounts are determined from a network of rain gauges. Raindrop sizes and densities determine rainfall intensity.

To Do: Simply set the straight-sided cans out in the rain at various locations. Use a plastic ruler marked in 32nds of an inch as a measuring stick. You may need to trim the end of the ruler so that the bottom is the zero point.

With these simple rain gauges, study local precipitation patterns. How do rainfall totals vary near buildings or trees or in the garden? How does the wind direction affect the amount collected in various gauges? Over a season, what wind direction brings the most rainfall? the least? the most intense?

Briefly set a shallow pan of flour out in the rain. Measure the diameters of the flour-coated drops. What is the range of sizes? How do sizes vary with the storm duration, intensity, and total rainfall?

Go Fly a Kite. Literally. Gauge wind speeds at different heights by flying a kite. Estimate the surface wind speed by using the Beaufort Scale of Wind Force, given earlier in this chapter. Climb a tree to experience the nuances between "light," "gentle," "moderate," "fresh," and "strong" breezes among the branches. From your perch read "The Wind" by Robert Louis Stevenson. Climb down before you're blown down.

CHAPTER 8

Climate, Weather, and You: Getting Along Together

Climate is not just the long-term average of the weather, but also the result of interactions between the atmospheric processes and the land surfaces, ice and snow cover, oceans, and the living world.

The relationship between climate and humans is a two-way interaction in which we humans both avoid weather hazards and utilize the natural resources controlled by the climate, while both adapting to the existing climate and attempting to modify it more to our liking.

Such physiological adaptations as metabolism, skin pigmentation, red cell content of blood, genetic immunities and tolerances to some diseases, as well as variations in body forms, have allowed us to occupy all of the earth's climate zones—a feat accomplished by few other organisms. Behavioral adaptations of clothing, shelter, plant and animal domestication, food production and storage, and modern energy, transportation, and communication systems help us survive in all climates.

In this chapter, we focus on a few of the effects weather has on human activities and health—and a few of the effects our activities have on the weather, climate, and health of the planet.

HOW WEATHER AND CLIMATE AFFECT HUMANS

Weather affects us in ways both large and small, but knowing these effects permits us to prepare for them. Over the climate average of a few decades, we may delineate floodplains, adjust energy distribution networks, or prepare for natural disasters. We may prepare our gardens based on the average date of the last killing frost, or purchase flood insurance based on probabilities for just such an event.

Over a season's length, we can approximate the amount of heating oil required, or the needed capacity of an air conditioner. We may vaccinate against a new strain of influenza, or vacation in a warmer and dryer locale. We may predict market prices of fruit and vegetable crops, and adjust transportation and distribution networks of the produce.

Over the matter of a few hours, we may decide to carry an umbrella or cancel an outdoor concert based on a probability-of-precipitation forecast. We may dress to avoid the wind and possible frostbite, or drink more water and avoid hyperthermia.

Health Effects. Weather has a direct and profound effect on human health. Mortality rates increase during heat and cold waves; conception rates are higher in winter than in summer; illnesses are transmitted by airborne viruses; even work performance, learning, and emotional well-being are tied to specific weather events and patterns. Indirectly, weather impacts human health by

WEATHER EFFECTS ON HEALTH

Weather Condition/Component	Known Effects on Human Health
Cold weather	Hypothermia, frostbite; leads to respiratory diseases, including pneumonia, bronchitis, influenza, and respiratory viral infections; *cold and dry:* impairs lung functions; *cold and damp:* aggravates rheumatism
Hot weather	Hyperthermia; increases mortalities attributed to other causes; aggravates renal and circulatory afflictions; *hot and dry:* heat stroke; leads to dehydration; *hot and damp:* heat exhaustion; impairs human performance; increases skin infections; increases stress; conducive to growth and prevalence of pathogens; increases range and population densities of disease-carrying organisms (mosquitoes, ticks, fleas, etc.)
Severe or extreme weather	Direct and indirect mortalities and injuries; increases stroke-related impairments; aggravates stress disorders; slows human responses
Sunlight	Excess causes sunburn; leads to skin cancer; long-term deprivation impairs emotional well-being and leads to depression
Airborne microorganisms	Cause infections
Particulate matter	Causes breathing difficulties, especially in those suffering from heart or lung disease
Sulfur oxides (SOx)	Cause smog; aggravate upper-respiratory disease and heart conditions; cause eye and throat irritations
Carbon monoxide (CO)	Reduces the oxygen-carrying capacity of the blood; low concentrations can impair mental abilities and affect those with heart and respiratory ailments; high concentrations cause death
Ozone(O_3)	Causes nose and throat irritations, impairs breathing
Nitrogen oxides (NOx)	Causes eye, throat, and lung irritations

affecting crop yields, food supplies, and disease-carrying pest populations. The major known effects of broad weather conditions are summarized in the preceeding table.

Exposure to Wind and Cold. Whenever the mercury drops below 58°F or so, our internal temperature also starts to drop. To compensate, we have several responses. Increasing our metabolic rate by eating food or by increasing muscular activity are two voluntary things we can do.

But the body itself (with no help from the thinking part of us) keeps its own thermostat; even if we wanted to be cold, signals are sent in spite of us to the muscles to increase tensing, resulting in shivering. Involuntary shivering increases body metabolism to help maintain a higher body temperature.

Vasoconstriction also kicks into gear when the temperature drops. Vasoconstriction is the narrowing of peripheral blood vessels in the body to reduce blood flow to the outer layers of skin, thereby reducing heat loss.

Add a breeze to the cooler temps and the body loses heat much more quickly. It's a familiar experience that windy days are much colder than calm days of the same temperature. Air is such a poor conductor of heat that if no wind is blowing and we are not moving, a thin layer of warm air forms next to the skin and we may feel quite comfortable. But with air in motion, the wind specializes in heat loss by convection.

The *wind chill index* relates how cold it really is (the actual temperature) to how cold it feels (the apparent temperature due to the cooling power of the wind). Its calculated values, displayed in the following chart, are approximations because of variations of individual body sizes, shapes, and metabolic rates. But it is also an approximation because it is based on the cooling rate of a nude body in the shade—not a practical daily application for most of us. Nonetheless, many of us do not dress warmly enough to compensate for the wind chill: Heed it and prepare properly.

Exposure to Heat and Humidity. A one-time *Nancy* comic strip starts off with Sluggo saying that he can't believe how hot the day is.

"Yeah, but it's not the heat that bothers me," Nancy responds as she dives into the air and swims through it, "it's the humidity."

At times it seems that that just might be possible. Summertime in the east could definitely be more tolerable without the excessive humidity.

Because our bodies cool by evaporation, the relative humidity affects how cool we feel. If the relative humidity is low (say 10 to 25 percent), perspiration on the skin absorbs heat from the body and evaporates into the air, carrying away body heat. However, as humidity (the vapor pressure) increases, the rate of evaporation decreases. Hence the perspiration does not readily evapo-

WIND CHILL INDEX

Temp. °F	Wind Speed (mph)								
	calm	5	10	15	20	25	30	35	40
30	32	30	25	21	18	15	12	10	−7
25	27	25	20	16	12	8	5	2	−1
20	23	20	14	9	5	1	−2	−6	−9
15	18	15	9	4	−1	−5	−10	−14	−18
10	13	10	4	−2	−8	−13	−18	−23	−28
5	8	5	−2	−9	−15	−20	−26	−32	−38
0	3	0	−7	−15	−22	−28	−35	−42	−49
−5	0	−3	−11	−18	−26	−33	−41	−48	−56
−10	−6	−10	−19	−28	−36	−45	−54	−63	
−15	−11	−15	−24	−35	−43	−53	−64		
−20	−16	−20	−30	−41	−52	−63			

How cold it feels

rate but stays on the skin, creating that warm, sticky feeling. Body heat does not dissipate through evaporational cooling but builds up instead, making us feel even hotter than what we would expect to feel at that temperature.

The *heat index*, the counterpart to the wind chill index, relates how warm it feels with high humidity compared to a dry environment. Various other indices have been developed to address this discomfort we all feel; they include the apparent temperature, the heat stress index, the "humiture," the "humidex," even a "summer simmer index." Some account for effects of solar radiation, wind speed, and barometric pressure on the human condition.

A temperature of 90°F at 30 percent relative humidity is bad enough, you would think, but couple that heat with 90 percent relative humidity, and it feels like 122 degrees! For most people, no discomfort is felt until an apparent temperature of 85°F is reached. Increased discomfort is felt at an apparent 90–93°F. At an apparent temperature of 100–105°F the possibility of heat stroke surfaces, and a prolonged exposure at apparent temperatures over 120, the danger of heat stroke is very real.

Maybe you'd rather not be reminded of how hot it feels. Albert Schweitzer, who did not keep a thermometer with him in equatorial Africa, declared that if he knew how hot it was, he couldn't stand it. So you may or may not want to use this chart. But if you do, remember, it's not the heat—it's the humidity.

HEAT INDEX

Temp. °F	Relative Humidity (%)									
	10	20	30	40	50	60	70	80	90	100
70	65	66	67	68	69	70	70	71	71	72
75	70	72	73	74	75	76	77	78	79	80
80	75	77	78	79	81	82	85	86	88	91
85	80	82	84	86	88	90	93	97	102	108
90	85	87	90	93	96	100	106	113	122	
95	90	93	96	101	107	114	124	136		
100	95	99	104	110	120	132	144			
105	100	105	113	123	135	149				

How hot it feels

Exposure to Sunlight. The ultraviolet (UV) portion of insolation is largely absorbed by the ozone layer in the stratosphere. The little bit that reaches the earth's surface, however, is known as *biologically active UV* (UVB) and is what causes sunburns and other skin problems. Heavy UV exposure releases chemical substances in the body causing local inflammations and suppresses certain immune responses. Chronic sunburn and long-term exposure to the sun can lead to cataracts and result in premature aging of the skin. UV-induced damage to DNA has been linked to cancer and genetic mutations.

The exposure to UV radiation varies with the time of day, season of the year, latitude, altitude, amount of clouds, as well as the length of time spent outdoors, the surface environment, and skin pigmentation. While clouds cut the exposure, they do not screen all the UV, and even cloudy days present some risk. Water, sand, and snow all reflect UV rays, increasing exposure. People with fairer skin are more at risk than those with darker skin.

The following precautions can help minimize exposure and the long-term risks:

Minimize sun exposure between 10 A.M. and 4 P.M.

Wear clothing that covers your body and a wide-brimmed hat that shades your face and neck.

Avoid unnecessary exposure from sunlamps and tanning devices.

Apply a sunscreen with SPF 15 or higher to all exposed areas sufficiently for protection, especially after swimming, perspiring, or sunbathing, even on cloudy days. Apply liberally and frequently to children older than six months.

Wear sunglasses that absorb the full UV spectrum in bright sunlight.

The *UV index,* developed by the National Weather Service and the Environmental Protection Agency, provides a way to help plan outdoor activities and prevent overexposure to the sun. The index values are developed using a computer model that relates forecasted ozone levels in the stratosphere to the amount and specific frequencies of UV reaching the ground. This is then correlated with the forecasted cloud coverage over 58 forecast cities, along with their elevations, to prepare forecasts of the likely levels of ultraviolet radiation at solar noon time the next day.

UV INDEX

Value	Exposure	Time to Burn	Precautions
0–2	Minimal	60 min.	Hat
3–4	Low	45 min.	Hat, sunscreen
5–6	Moderate	30 min.	Hat, sunscreen SPF 15
7–9	High	15–24 min.	Hat, sunscreen SPF 15 to 30, sunglasses; limit midday exposure
10+	Very high	10 min. or less	Hat, sunscreen SPF 30, sunglasses, protective clothing; avoid sun exposure 10 A.M.–3 P.M.

Exposure to Air Pollution. Anything not naturally occurring in a specific environment can be classified as a pollutant, and both natural processes and human activities release such foreign substances into air, water, and soil. Air pollution refers to contaminants present in such quantities or duration to be injurious to human, plant, or animal life, or detrimental to comfort. Primary pollutants of industrial chemicals and suspended solid or liquid matter, called particulates, enter the atmosphere directly; secondary pollutants form in the atmosphere in chemical reactions with water vapor and atmospheric gases and/or with primary pollutants.

FACT: Lichens live only in areas of good air quality; they are generally not found in cities.

The *U.S. air quality index* is a measure of the concentrations of several contaminants in the air, monitored over specific time intervals, each with respect to the threshold of human sensitivity. The index alerts the public to combined expected levels of pollutants, their detrimental effects, and recommended changes in behavior.

Socioeconomic Effects. As humans learn more about weather and climate, we try to use that knowledge to the betterment of society at large.

Natural Disaster and Land Use. Thanks to studies of severe weather events, we are better able to know what to expect if a hurricane is forecasted to make landfall in a populated area, or if a tornado has been reported in the county, or if a winter storm warning has been issued. We are better prepared for natural disasters in terms of adequate supplies and improved construction techniques, building codes, warning systems, and evacuation routes.

Floodplains have been delineated, permitting governments to regulate land use for the overall public good. Knowledge of rainfall frequency and duration and other climatic data is used for estimating runoff and for determining such things as the required diameters of culvert pipes and volumes of storm drainage systems. With a better understanding of climatic causes and effects comes better use of the land.

The effect of the past temperature on some quantity, such as plant growth, electrical generation, or fuel consumption, may be assessed with a climatic measure called the *degree day*. A measure of the departure from the mean daily temperature from a given standard, one degree day is equal to one degree above or below the standard during one day.

Heating degree days and *cooling degree days* are accumulated over a season to determine trends in fuel and power consumption, and are obtained by adding or subtracting the average daily temperature to or from a standard of 65°F. Thus, a day with a high of 50°F and a low of 30°F with an average of 40° has 25 heating degree days.

Because urban areas create and retain heat, a variety of practices are being instituted to help with cooling such as light-colored structures and road surfaces, and tree-planting. Energy conservation is being promoted by building designs and orientations that maximize daylight lighting and passive solar energy; by windows that reflect infrared heat while insulating against heat loss; and by better structural insulation and energy-efficient appliances. Such are a few of the benefits of applying climatic wisdom to efficient living.

Precipitation Forecasts. The forecasts known as probability-of-precipitation statements have been standard language of the National Weather Service since the mid-1960s. Popular with the public, but confusing, proba-

U.S. AIR QUALITY INDEX

Air Pollutant Levels (micrograms per cubic meter)

Value	Description	24 hr. Particulates	24 hr. SO_2	8 hr. CO	1 hr. O_3	1 hr. NO_2	Effects & Suggested Actions
50	Good	75	80	5,000	118	?	No significant effects
100	Moderate	260	365	10,000	235	?	Some damage to materials and plants; human health not affected unless levels continue for many days
200	Unhealthful	375	800	17,000	400	1,130	Healthy persons notice irritations; those with lung or heart disease should reduce physical exertion
300	Very unhealthful	625	1,600	34,000	800	2,260	All persons notice lung irritations; high-risk persons have more symptoms and should stay indoors and reduce physical activity
400	Hazardous	875	2,100	46,000	1,000	3,000	All persons should avoid outdoor activity; high-risk persons should stay quietly indoors
500	Very hazardous	1,000	2,620	57,000	1,200	3,750	Normal activity impossible; all should remain indoors with windows and doors closed; special risk to elderly and those with heart and lung ailments

bility statements are based on numerical precision; they give no indications of amounts, durations, or intensities of rainfall.

The probabilities can be very useful to business and government in making decisions about activities that are sensitive to the weather. But few business or governmental operations know how to play the odds. Moreover, few people understand the specific definition of the probability forecast, resulting in much confusion and many interpretations. Here are five different ways that a forecast of a "30 percent chance of rain tonight" could be interpreted:

1. It will rain 30 percent of the time tonight.

2. There are three chances in ten that rain will fall sometime tonight.

3. Three-tenths of the forecast area will receive measurable rain in the forecast period.

4. There is a 30 percent chance a general rain will cover the entire area.

5. There is a 30 percent probability that any place in the forecast area will receive measurable rain (.01 inch or more) sometime during the forecast period.

The National Weather Service has adopted definition 5. The problem is that the public doesn't know the rules, and the Weather Service doesn't always stick to them. Furthermore, other terms in the probability forecast can add their own vagaries: What is "tonight"? Does a 50 percent chance "this afternoon and tonight" mean 50 percent this afternoon and another 50 percent chance during tonight? How about vague terms like "slight," "chance," and "occasional"? If the public misunderstands a forecast, it's simply wrong, even if it verifies exactly according to the definitions. Such is the challenge of the forecaster. And such is the challenge of the forecast users.

DEFINING THE PROBABLE

To help with the understanding, of precipitation forecasts, here are a few of the more commonly used (and defined) forecast terms.

Percent of Probability	Uncertainty Expression	Equivalent Areal Coverage
10–20	Slight chance	Isolated or few or widely scattered
30–50	Chance	Scattered
60–70	Likely	Numerous
80–100	None used	None used

The terms *brief, occasional, intermittent,* and *frequent* are used to denote duration.

HOW HUMANS AFFECT THE WEATHER AND THE CLIMATE

The very innovations that have allowed humans to prosper in all climates have altered the climate itself. Such consequences may be positive or negative, or both. There remain two great unanswered questions: 1. Can we avoid changing the climate? 2. If not, can we adapt to the changing conditions? Presented here, with hopes for positive resolutions, are brief descriptions of a few of the most pressing issues of climatic change.

Weather Modification. Weather modification projects seek to improve existing weather conditions for specific results. The simplest projects dissipate cold fogs at airports to improve visibility. Upslope fogs and clouds may be treated to increase rainfall or snowfall in dry regions. More complex projects attempt to seed convective clouds with silver iodide compounds or other particles to increase precipitation or decrease hail. The most elaborate plans attempt to diminish the fury of hurricanes and midlatitude cyclones.

Such projects are noble exercises, but many are filled with uncertainty. Because no two clouds are alike, and the atmosphere remains in constant fluid motion, it is extremely difficult to qualify and quantify any results. Perhaps the end result may have occurred without any intervention. Another issue is that weather systems move: Some people may want the changes, others may not. Changes in precipitation may affect the long-term climate, which in turn affects the land, animals, and people. Are we prepared for such far-reaching consequences?

Heat Island Effect. Perhaps the clearest example of inadvertent human modification of the climate is the characteristic warmth generated by a city, compared with its rural surroundings. Termed the *urban heat island effect,* its increase for a large city under clear, calm conditions may be as much as 18°F at the surface during the day, lowering to a minimum value at night.

Man-made alterations to the natural environment account for the increases in the city temperatures as well as other modifications to the overall climate. The predominance of heat-absorbing surfaces like concrete, brick, and asphalt, combined with a reduction in transpiring vegetation, is a primary cause. The canyon structure of tall buildings, which enhances warming by multiple reflections from its glass, also reduces heat dissipation by preventing mixing winds. Rainfall is channeled as runoff and therefore is not available to contribute to evaporational cooling, and buildings and vehicles contribute waste heat.

WEATHER IN THE CITY

Cities	As Compared with Rural Areas
Temperature, annual mean	2° to 5°F higher
Relative humidity, annual mean	6% lower
Cloud cover	5 to 10% more
Precipitation, total amounts	5 to 10% more
Wind speed, annual mean	20 to 30% lower
Duration of sunshine	5 to 15% less

Desertification. *Desertification* is defined by the United Nations as the "diminution or destruction of the biological potential of the land [which] can lead ultimately to desert-like conditions." Causes can include increasing populations, people abandoning nomadic traditions to settle in towns, new and inappropriate technologies, more livestock, deforestation, and overcultivation.

Scientists disagree, however, on the causes and processes of degradation, the amount of land affected, and the extent to which the changes are natural or human-induced. One thing is clear, however: Climate, life, and the environment are inextricably linked.

Acid Deposition. Complex chemical reactions in the air produce acidic compounds as pollutants combine with atmospheric moisture and gases. Pollution from motor vehicles and coal-fired power plants account for the three most common and serious acids: sulfur dioxides, nitrogen oxides, and volatile organic carbons.

Acid rain occurs when these compounds are taken from the air by rainfall. Because they may also be removed from the atmosphere by fog or snow, or even by dry particles or gases that react with moisture on the surface to form acids, an all-encompassing term for the process is *acid deposition.*

It is thought that many pollutants interact in such a way to be more harmful as a group than individually. In severely affected areas, buildings, statues, gravestones, and other exposed structures and materials erode at alarming rates. Lakes may be devoid of life, soil nutrients depleted, and field crops stunted.

FACT: An acid level of pH 3.5 to 4.0 is lethal to salmon and trout, inhibits seed germination, and injures leaves.

Mitigation of acid deposition requires emissions reduction programs along with environmental impact assessments. And society faces a big question: What are the acceptable trade-offs between less-acidic rain because of stricter laws, and the higher industrial productivity and lower consumer costs that might be possible without the laws?

Ozone Depletion. The ozone layer is a thin layer of triatomic oxygen (O_3) at a level of 7.5 to 30 miles up in the stratosphere. If it were concentrated to a uniform depth, it would only be about 3 millimeters thick. So little, but so important, ozone absorbs 99 percent of the harmful ultraviolet light entering our atmosphere.

In recent years, a "hole" in the ozone layer has temporarily appeared over Antarctica during the southern hemisphere spring. Rather than being a literal hole, it is a large area of the stratosphere with low amounts of ozone. At its worst, about 9 to 12 miles above the surface, more than 60 percent is lost. Ozone levels have also seasonally dropped 5 to 10 percent over much of the other six continents.

The annual loss of ozone is connected to reactive chlorine in the stratosphere, primarily derived from man-made chlorine-containing compounds such as methyl chloroform, a solvent; carbon tetrachloride, an industrial chemical; and chloroflourocarbons (CFCs), used as refrigerants, solvents, and foam-blowing agents in making polystyrene (foam plastic). CFCs were also formerly used as propellents in aerosol cans. Halons used in fire extinguishers, and methyl bromide, a soil fumigant, contain bromine, which is chemically similar to chlorine. Natural sources contribute about 15 percent of the chlorine in the air, primarily from large fires and certain types of marine life.

All of these compounds are stable enough in the air to be transported by the winds into the stratosphere, where they finally break down with exposure to ultraviolet light. As they do, they release chlorine atoms, which combine with single oxygen atoms from the ozone to form chlorine monoxide (ClO) and ordinary diatomic oxygen (O_2). This reaction destroys ozone molecules at the rate of 1:100,000—faster than they are naturally created.

Reductions in the ozone levels lead to higher levels of ultraviolet radiation at the earth's surface. This radiation can increase risks of malignant melanoma and cataracts in humans and upset marine ecosystems by inhibiting photosynthesis in phytoplankton.

International agreements starting in 1987 have set goals for CFC reductions, which have been met, and chlorine levels are now below the maximum allowed tropospheric limits. Non-harmful substitutes for CFCs are increasing in use, and stratospheric chlorine will shortly peak, then steadily fall. Assuming continued compliance, normal ozone levels should completely recover by natural processes by about 2050.

Global Warming. We still don't know whether the detected temperature increases in the global climate (about half a degree celsius, or almost 1 degree Fahrenheit in the past one hundred years) is the result of human activities or of natural causes. Global climate models are still no match for the incalculable range of interrelated causes and effects in the real world's hugely complex atmosphere—and its equally involved interactions with the sun, oceans, and land.

Just one of the big challenges in modeling is estimating the precise effect of clouds, and the temperature equilibrium they help set between the earth and the atmosphere. Clouds absorb heat, which warms the surrounding air; but they also reflect sunlight, which cools the surrounding air. With fewer clouds, more insolation reaches the ground, and temperatures rise, which leads to greater evaporation, which leads to more clouds, which cuts the amount of insolation reaching the ground, which lowers temperatures: a self-regulating cycle.

Atmospheric nitrogen and oxygen, which make up 98 percent of the air, absorb virtually no infrared radiation from the sun, allowing it to escape to space. Water vapor and carbon dioxide, however, do absorb the radiation. The increasing concentrations of carbon dioxide—and other heat-absorbing gases of methane, nitrous oxide, and CFCs—tend to raise the temperature, and are blamed on such human activities as burning fossil fuels, clear-cutting rain forests, and raising cattle and rice. On the other hand, the presence of sulfur dioxide in the atmosphere from power plants tends to increase cloud cover, which contributes to cooling.

How much of the noted temperature increase is due to natural fluctuations or cycles in ocean currents, or atmospheric patterns, or solar activity? How much is due to more precise and extensive observations in the past few years? Quantitative records (back to 1880) only exist for a miniscule fraction of the atmosphere's existence, which we do know has fluctuated quite widely in past eras. As recently as 1940–1977, global temperatures markedly declined, and there was talk of a return to the ice ages.

Conflicting measurements add to the uncertainty. According to land and ocean surface observations, 1997 was 0.19°C warmer than the 1982–1991 average. But according to satellite observations by NOAA's Microwave Sounding Unit, the year was 0.08°C *cooler* than the average. It is possible that both measurements are technically correct, since they measure different things to determine the total amount of heat. If so, what does it really mean?

While the research and the debate continues we need not wait to implement such beneficial practices and overall cooling effects as greater energy conservation measures, lower pollution emissions, and widespread development of renewable energy resources. This we can do, as we continue to learn how the fierce and favorable atmosphere continually interacts with the interfering and interdependent life on earth.

OBSERVATIONS AND ACTIVITIES

Measure the Acidity of Rainwater. Rainwater can be tested to determine how acidic or alkaline it is, and the result used to judge its effects on living organisms.

Materials: Some pH indicator test paper strips, rain gauge, small clean plastic or glass container, pencil, paper.

To Know: All acids contain hydrogen; the more hydrogen, the stronger the acid. The pH (potential of Hydrogen) is a measure of the degree of acidity of a solution. Based on a 14-point scale, with 7 as neutral, solutions with a pH below 7 are acidic and those above 7 are basic, or alkaline. The scale is logarithmic, which means there is a tenfold difference between the whole numbers. A solution that has a pH of 2 is ten times more acidic than one of 3 and one hundred times as acidic as one with 4.

To Do: Place a small sample of collected rainwater in your test container and dip a 1 inch strip of the pH paper in it. Compare the color of the test strip to the color chart and record the pH.

Note the sizes and directions of the storms that produce precipitation. How does pH vary with direction or size of the storm?

During the passage of a long-lasting storm, measure the pH at regular intervals. Does it change with time?

Collect some snow, let it melt, and measure its pH. Does the pH of snow change with the depth of your sample? Is there a pattern to the pH of precipitation over the course of the year?

Test the pH of a nearby pond, lake, or stream. How can this be affected by a sudden spring melt of acidic snow deposited earlier? How would a limestone soil or streambed affect the results of acid deposition?

Research the News. Document examples of the two-way relationship between weather/climate and living organisms.

Materials: Newspapers, magazines, broadcasts, on-line publications.

To Know: Awareness is the first part of true environmental education. It leads to greater understanding of how all things are interrelated and interdependent and how to be effective in helping to solve problems.

To Do: Read, research, and assemble documentation of animal, plant, and human responses to the weather and climate, and their effects on it. Search for conflicting views and multiple interpretations and conclusions. Compare and contrast; keep an open mind; encourage and participate in further studies; be part of the solutions, not of the problems; always continue learning.

Get Personal with the Weather. Conduct interviews of several people whose professions are directly affected by the weather and climate, such as farmers, pilots, river navigators, construction workers, and so forth. How much does the livelihood of each person depend on the weather? What constitutes "good" weather? "Bad" weather? How does this opinion vary with the profession? What is each person's most memorable weather event? Why? What changes in the climate would be beneficial? Detrimental?

Use Less Energy. Keep a daily log of energy use at your home to observe daily and seasonal variations. Make daily readings of your gas and electric meters, and relate them to specific uses. Estimate the energy used in a hot shower vs. a hot bath. Record the amounts and costs of all fuels, and their total energy supply. Divide by the number of people in your household: How does your consumption compare to the local or national average?

Try some conservation measures: Add more insulation in the house, lower the thermostat, use public transportation, turn off unused appliances and lights, use a clothesline instead of a dryer, reuse and recycle products. You might also plant a row of trees as a windbreak for your house, compost food and vegetative wastes, stop fertilizing your lawn, plant a vegetable garden to meet your own food requirements. Consider installing some method of solar heating in your home. Ride a bike.

APPENDIX 1:
UNIT CONVERSION TABLES

LENGTH

1 kilometer	= 1,000 meters (m)
	= .62137 statute mile (mi)
	= .5399 nautical mile (n mi)
	= 3,281 feet (ft)
1 meter	= 100 centimeters (cm)
	= 3.28084 ft
	= 39.365568 inches (in)
1 centimeter	= 10 millimeters (mm)
	= .394 in
1 micron (μ)	= 10^{-6} m
	= .001 mm
	= .00004 in.
1 statute mile	= 1.60934 km
	= .86898 n mi
	= 5,280 ft

1 foot	= .304799 m
1 inch	= 2.54 cm
1 nautical mile	= 1.85199 km = 1,851.9962 m
	= 1.15078 mi
	= 6,076 ft
	= 1 minute of latitude arc (')

1 degree of latitude arc (°) = 60 minutes of latitude arc = 60 n mi

VELOCITY

1 kilometer/hr	= .2778 m/sec
	= .62137 mph
	= 54.68 ft/min
	= .5396 knots (nautical miles per hour)
1 meter/sec	= 3.60 km/hr
	= 2.24 mph
	= 3.28 ft/sec
	= 1.94 knots (kt)
1 mph	= 88 ft/min.
	= 1.46 ft/sec
	= 1.60934 km/h
	= .447 m/sec
	= .868 kt
1 knot	= 1 nautical mph
	= 1.15 statute mph
	= 1.852 km/hr
	= .514 m/sec

HEAT

$$°C = \tfrac{5}{9}(°F-32) \qquad °F = \tfrac{9}{5}°C + 32 \qquad K = °C + 273.15$$

°C	°F	°C	°F	°C	°F	°C	°F
−50	−58	−25	−13	0	32	25	77
−45	−49	−20	−4	5	41	30	86
−40	−40	−15	5	10	50	35	95
−35	−31	−10	14	15	59	40	104
−30	−22	−5	23	20	68	45	122

PRESSURE

1 standard atmosphere	= 1013.25 mb
	= 14.70 lb/in^2
	= 760 mm mercury (Hg)
	= 29.92 in. Hg

1 millibar (mb)	= .0145 lb/in^2
	= .0295 in. Hg
	= .75 mm Hg
	= 100 newtons/m^2 (N/m^2)
	= 100 pascals (Pa)
	= 1 hectopascal (hPa)

1 in. Hg	= 25.4 mm Hg
	= 33.86 mb
	= 33.86 hPa
	= .033 atm

TIME

Greenwich Mean Time (GMT) = Universal Time (UT) = Zulu Time (Z) = the mean solar time at the prime meridian (0° longitude).

	Pacific	Mountain	Central	Eastern	Atlantic	GMT
Standard	−8 hr	−7 hr	−6 hr	−5 hr	−4 hr	0
Daylight Savings	−7 hr	−6 hr	−5 hr	−4 hr	−3 hr	0

Appendix 2:
Selected Bibliography

GENERAL METEOROLOGY

Anthes, R. A., J. Cahir, A. B. Fraser, and H. A. Panofski. *The Atmosphere.* 3d ed. Columbus: Charles E. Merrill Publishing, 1981.

Battan, Louis J. *Fundamentals of Meteorology.* Englewood Cliffs, N.J.: Prentice Hall, 1984.

Burroughs, W. J., B. Crowder, T. Robertson, E. Vallier-Talbot, and R. Whitaker. *The Nature Company Guides: Weather.* New York: Time-Life Books, 1996.

Posey, Carl A. *Wind & Weather.* New York: Reader's Digest, 1994.

Schaefer, Vincent J., and John A. Day Houghton. *A Field Guide to the Atmosphere.* Boston: Mifflin Co., 1981.

Williams, Jack. *The Weather Book.* 2d ed. New York: Vintage Books, 1997.

OPTICAL PHENOMENA

Greenler, Robert. *Rainbows, Halos, and Glories.* Cambridge: Cambridge University Press, 1980.

Humphreys, W. J. *Physics of the Air.* New York: Dover Publications, 1964.

Meinel, Aden and Marjorie. *Sunsets, Twilights, and Evening Skies.* Cambridge: Cambridge University Press, 1983.

Minnaert, M. *The Nature of Light & Color in the Open Air.* New York: Dover Publications, 1954.

O'Connell, D. J. K. *The Green Flash and Other Low Sun Phenomena*. New York: Interscience Publishers, 1958.

Scorer, Richard. *Clouds of the World*. Mechanicsburg, Pa.: Stackpole Books, 1972.

Tape, Walter. *Atmospheric Halos*. Washington, D.C.: American Geophysical Union, 1994.

WEATHERLORE AND WEATHER-RELATED NATURAL HISTORY

Dolan, Edward F. *The Old Farmer's Almanac Book of Weatherlore*. Dublin, N.H.: Yankee Books, 1988.

Lee, Albert, ed. *Weather Wisdom*. New York: Doubleday & Co., 1990.

Page, Robin. *Weather Forecasting the Country Way*. New York: Summit Books, 1977.

Sloane, Eric. *Folklore of American Weather*. New York: Duell, Sloan, and Pearce, 1963.

Thomas, Helen Sattler. *Nature's Weather Forecasters*. New York: Nelson Publishers, 1978.

HISTORICAL WEATHER, CLIMATE, AND CLIMATE CHANGE

Bair, Frank, ed. *The Weather Almanac*. 6th ed. Detroit: Gale Research, 1992.

Detwyler, Thomas. *Man's Impact on Environment*. New York: McGraw-Hill, 1971.

Edwin, Dean, ed. *The Challenge of Global Warming*. Washington, D.C.: Abrahamson Island Press, 1989.

Ludlum, David M. *The Weather Factor*. New York: Houghton Mifflin, 1984.

Lydolph, Paul E. *The Climate of the Earth*. Totowa, N.J.: Roman and Allanheld, 1985.

Schneider, Stephen, and Randi Londer. *The Coevolution of Climate & Life*. San Francisco: Sierra Club Books, 1984.

SPECIAL TOPICS AND APPLICATIONS

Dabberdt, Walter F. *Weather for Outdoorsmen*. New York: Charles Scribner's Sons, 1981.

Dennis, Jerry. *It's Raining Frogs & Fishes*. New York: Harper Perennial, 1993.

Doesken, Nolan, and Arthur Judson. *The Snow Booklet*. 2d ed. Fort Collins, Colo.: Colorado State University, 1997.

Kreh, Lefty. *The L. L. Bean Guide to Outdoor Photography*. New York: Random House, 1988.

McClung, David, and Peter Schaerer. *The Avalanche Handbook.* Seattle: The Mountaineers, 1993.

Roth, Charles E. *The Sky Observer's Handbook.* New York: Phalarope Books, 1986.

Simonds, Calvin. *The Weather-wise Gardener.* Emmaus, Pa.: Rodale Press, 1983.

Townsend, Sallie, and Virginia Ericson. *Boating Weather: How to Predict It, What to Do About It.* New York: David McKay Company, 1978.

Wagner, Ronald, and Bill Adler Jr. *The Weather Sourcebook.* Old Saybrook, Conn.: The Globe Pequot Press, 1994.

ACTIVITIES

Bohren, Craig. *Clouds in a Glass of Beer.* New York: John Wiley & Sons, 1987.

Hillcourt, William. *The New Field Book of Nature Activities & Hobbies.* New York: G. P. Putnam's Sons, 1970.

Mandell, Muriel. *Simple Weather Experiments with Everyday Materials.* New York: Sterling Publishing Co., 1990.

Mogil, H. Michael, and Barbara Levin. *The Amateur Meteorologist: Explorations and Investigations.* New York: Franklin Watts, 1993.

Trowbridge, Leslie. *Experiments in Meteorology.* New York: Doubleday & Co., 1973.

APPENDIX 3:
RESOURCES

WEATHER INSTRUMENTS AND EQUIPMENT

Davis Instruments
3465 Diablo Avenue
Hayward, CA 94545
800-678-3669
info@davisnet.com

Downeaster Mfg. Co.
574 Main Street, Route 6A
Dennis, Cape Cod, MA 02638
800-253-4878
www.downeaster.com

Edmund Scientific
101 East Gloucester Pike
Barrington, NJ 08007
800-728-6999
www.edsci.com

Maximum Wind and Weather
Instruments
30 Barnet Boulevard
New Bedford, MA 02745
508-995-2200
sales.maximum@imtra.com

Novalynx Corp.
P.O. Box 240
Grass Valley, CA 95945
800-321-3577
nova@novalynx.com

Peet Bros. Company
1308 Doris Avenue
Ocean, NJ 07712
800-872-7338
peetbros@peetbros.com

RainWise
25 Federal Street
Bar Harbor, ME 04609
800-762-5723
sales@rainwise.com

Robert E. White Instruments
34 Commercial Wharf
Boston, MA 02110
800-992-3045
www.robertwhite.com

Sensor Instruments Co.
41 Terrell Park Drive
Concord, NH 03301
800-633-1033
sensor@seninsco.com

Texas Weather Instruments
5942 Abrams Road, #113
Dallas, TX 75231
800-284-0245
txweathr@iadfw.net

Wind & Weather
P.O. Box 2320
Mendocino, CA 95460
800-922-9463
fax: 707-964-1278

WEATHER RELATED PRODUCTS AND SERVICES

Carolina Biological Supply
2700 York Road
Burlington, NC 27215
800-547-1733
www.carolina.com

Data Transmission Network
    Corporation
9110 West Dodge Road, Suite 200
Omaha, NE 68114
800-610-0777
www.dtn.com

Educational Images Ltd.
P.O. Box 3456, West Side
Elmira, NY 14905
800-527-4264

Encyclopedia Britannica
310 South Michigan Avenue
Chicago, IL 60604
800-621-3900
www.eb.com

Everyday Weather Project
SUNY College at Brockport
Brockport, NY 14420
716-395-2352
jzollweg@vortex.weather.
    brockport.edu

Fascinating Electronics
31525 Canaan Road
Deer Island, OR 97054
503-397-1222
fax: 503-397-1191

How the Weatherworks
1522 Baylor Avenue
Rockville, MD 20850
301-762-7669
www.weatherworks.com

L'Softworks Ltd.
7357 Moonlight Lane
Eden Prairie, MN 55346
612-934-8069
wxbase@juno.com

National Archives Fulfillment
    Center
8700 Edgeworth Drive
Capitol Heights, MD 20743
301-763-1896

National Center for Atmospheric
    Research
Information Services
P.O. Box 3000
Boulder, CO 80307
303-497-8600

National Weather Association
6704 Wolke Court
Montgomery, AL 36116
334-213-0388

OFS WeatherFax
6404 Lakerest Court
Raleigh, NC 27612
919-847-4545

Ward's Natural Science
    Establishment
5100 West Henrietta Road
Rochester, NY 14692
and
815 Fiero Lane
San Luis Obispo, CA 93403
800-962-2660
www.wardsci.com

WeatherDisc Associates
4584 NE 89th Street
Seattle, WA 98115
206-524-4314
fax: 206-433-1162

WEATHER AND CLIMATOLOGICAL DATA

Accu-Weather
385 Science Park Road
State College, PA 16803
814-237-0309
info@accuwx.com
www.accuweather.com

Climate Prediction Center
World Weather Building
5200 Auth Road, Room 800
Washington, D.C. 20233
301-763-4670
www.nnic.noaa.gov/altindex.html

CNN Weather
www.cnn.com/weather/index.html

National Climatic Data Center
151 Patton Avenue, Room 120
Asheville, NC 28801
828-271-4800
www.ncdc.noaa.gov/ol/ncdc.html

National Hurricane Center Tropical
    Prediction Center
11691 S.W. 17th Street
Miami, FL 33165
305-229-4470
www.nhc.noaa.gov

National Severe Storms Laboratory
1313 Halley Circle
Norman, OK 73069

National Weather Service
NOAA Weather Radio
8060 13th Street, Gramax Building
Silver Spring, MD 20910
301-427-7622
www.nws.noaa.gov

NWS Interactive Weather Informa-
    tion Network
iwim.nws.noaa.gov/iwin/main.html

NOAA Climate Diagnostics Center
325 Broadway
Boulder, CO 80303
fax: 303-497-7013
www.cdc.noaa.gov

The NOAA Weather Page
www.esdim.noaa.gov/weather_page
    .html

StormFax Weather Services
www.stormfax.com

The Weather Channel
www.weather.com

USA Today Weather Index
www.usatoday.com/weather/
    windex.htm

Weather Science Hotlist
sln.fi.edu/tfi/hotlists/weather.html

World Wide Weather on the
    Internet
www.weather.net/fn/fsu.weather.
    html

PERIODICALS AND BULLETINS

Daily Weather Maps
Climate Prediction Center
4700 Silver Hill Road, Room 811
Washington, D.C. 20233
301-763-8000

Mariner's Weather Log
(also miscellaneous other
    documents)
Superintendent of Documents
U.S. Government Printing Office
Washington, D.C. 20402
202-512-1800
Ordering address:
P.O. Box 371954
Pittsburgh, PA 15250

Weatherwise
1319 Eighteenth Street, NW
Washington, D.C. 20036-1802
800-365-9753
subs@heldref.org

ORGANIZATIONS

American Meteorological Society
45 Beacon Street
Boston, MA 02108
617-226-2425
www.ametsoc.org

National Weather Association
440 Stamp Road, Room 404
Temple Hills, MD 20748
301-899-3784

Mount Washington Observatory
1 Washington Street
Gorham, NH 03581
603-356-8345
www.mountwashington.org

Texas Severe Storm Association
506 Elliot Street
Arlington, TX 76013

World Meteorological Organization
Information and Public Affairs
    Office
41, Avenue Giuseppe – Matta –
    1211
Geneva 2, Switzerland
(041 22) 730-8314
fax: (041 22) 733-2829
www.wmo.ch/